There and Then

There
and
Then

A Vermont Childhood

Olive Pitkin

FITHIAN PRESS

SANTA BARBARA, 1997

Published by Fithian Press
A division of Daniel and Daniel, Publishers, Inc.
Post Office Box 1525
Santa Barbara, CA 93102

Book design: Eric Larson

LIBRARY OF CONGRESS CATALOGING-IN-PUBLICATION DATA
Pitkin, Olive.
    There and then : a Vermont childhood / by Olive Pitkin
      p. cm.
    ISBN 1-56474-198-2 (alk. paper)
    1. Bennington (Vt.)—Social life and customs. 2. Pitkin, Olive—Childhood and
  youth. 3. Bennington (Vt.)—Biography. I. Title.
F59.4P58   1997
974.3'8042'092—dc20   96-9788
                                                              CIP

*For my children
and their children*

Contents

Introduction

I was born in 1923. Nobody knew yet that the world had begun with a big bang, and nobody was yet worried about the possibility that it might end with another one. The world of my childhood was, as a child's ought to be, small and stable.

What kept it small was isolation; not even radio connected us yet to the rest of mankind. My parents of course stayed abreast of the events of their time, but it was not considered the thing in those days to force large worrisome affairs on the attention of young children; such matters were not even discussed in our presence. We had the luxury of being ignorant—in fact, innocent—in fact, childish.

I grew up in a succession of Vermont towns, with Vermont fore-bears for five generations on both sides—that is nearly as long as there has been a Vermont—and New England ones behind them again for nearly as long as there has been a New England. My child-hood was in no way remarkable for that time and place, but the time was quite a while back and the place (and its people) had a definite character; they seemed to me worth recapturing, if I could.

And quite aside from these specifics, I think any childhood any-where has a flavor of its own that has an appeal for most of us. We are, after all, from whatever different times and places, all cousins under the skin; and we like to hear at first hand how that most vivid and intense time of life went for someone else. In the reader there is, I suppose, some remnant of the child-that-was, that goes out to meet the author's child-that-used-to-be with eternal freshness of curiosity and greeting. At least I hope it is so in this case. In that hope, here is my child, to tell yours how it all was, and how it went for me, back there in the Green Mountains, in the olden days.

I make no claim to objective historical or sociological accuracy; this is not a scholarly treatise, but a dip into recollections sixty years and more in the making. My only research documents were *A History of Marshfield, Vt.*, written and published privately in 1941 by Ozias C. Pitkin and Fred E. Pitkin, and some pages of informal family reminiscence that my mother put together in her eighties. (I thought I owed it to my ancestors to get their names and dates right.) The rest came out of my head. I have written, honestly, about what I think I remember; but I was only a child, and greener than most, and memory is at best a clouded mirror. It is more than likely that I have got a few things wrong.

Be that as it may—hail, cousin! Come near, and listen.

WATCH HILL, RHODE ISLAND
JUNE, 1996

Shaker Hill

A LITTLE SOUTH OF BURLINGTON—Vermont's largest city, on the shore of Lake Champlain—there sits, in a quiet empty valley, the town of Starksboro, my mother's girlhood home. Starksboro is so small, and that time was so long ago, that its chief relations with the big world outside were conducted through Bristol, ten miles to the south, and Vergennes, fifteen miles to the southwest; I never heard my mother talk about any dealings with Burlington, or with Montpelier, the state capital, though neither one is more than thirty miles away.

Her home was not even in the town of Starksboro itself, which is tiny enough—a mere hamlet in fact—but on a sparsely-wooded granite hillside a good five miles to the northeast, called Shaker Hill. How it got this name I don't know; I never thought about its possible meaning until it was too late to ask. The Hill was populated, in those days, by Huletts and Fullers and Hills and Masons, who made a skimpy living raising small herds of dairy cows on the steep rock-strewn sides of the mountain and selling the milk down in town. My mother was Fannie Hulett; she was related to the other families on all sides. As I met them from time to time, and went in and out of their houses, these families seemed to me to be pretty much alike, but my mother drew sharp distinctions: there were those who only worked as day laborers on other men's farms; those who owned their own farms; and then those who held mortgages on their neighbors' farms. The Huletts were of this last group, and were said to be "known for their shrewdness and thrift." I believe it.

This family had not been on the Hill long. It was my mother's grandfather Asahel Hulett who came there in about 1880 from

Wallingford, sixty miles to the south, after a dispute with the town about taxes. It seems he was deeply offended because the town officials "wouldn't take his word" in some fiscal affair, and simply picked up and moved to Starksboro with his grown family. There, he apparently kept the chip on his shoulder in relation to money matters, resenting any imputation against his honesty and tending to express himself in decisive action. On one occasion, as my mother told it:

> My grandfather owed the storekeeper in Huntington Center, Edison Ellis, sixteen hundred dollars. I'm sure this was not for groceries. Probably some real estate deal in which Grandfather was always engaged. He offered Mr. Ellis a check, which the latter refused. So Grandfather, feeling his honor was impugned, in revenge got the whole sixteen hundred dollars in small change, put it into a twenty-five- or fifty-pound maple-sugar can, took it into the store on a Saturday night and dumped it on the counter. It being Saturday night there were plenty of witnesses in the store *and* no chance to bank the money till Monday. So by bedtime many of the townfolk knew Mr. Ellis had sixteen hundred dollars in cash in the house. The poor man and his wife had to sit up all Saturday and Sunday night to guard the money, to the great delight of the local wags.

A trick like that shows a man any Vermonter would be proud to call ancestor. The story adequately establishes my credentials as a Yankee on my mother's side.

The approach to my grandparents' house on Shaker Hill was for me like a pilgrimage, or the ascent to a giant's castle in a fairy story; you could tell, it seemed to me, that you were coming to a special place. From the town of Starksboro—to reach which we had already driven for five or six hours—we would enter on a narrow dirt road that wound up the side of the mountain with barely enough room for two cars or two wagons to pass (wagons being still, then, the standard transport and a car the rare exception). In many places, passing meant one of the vehicles had to back down, around invisible turns, to a place wide enough to get out of the way.

The grade was steep and the hillside, near the road, was heavily wooded; it was dark under the trees, even on a bright day. There was no fence of any kind protecting us from the considerable drop-off to the left or the massive, looming gray rocks on the right; to me a fall or a collision seemed inevitable from moment to moment. I never outgrew my dread on that road. The Model T took the whole climb in first gear, with a whining, moaning sound that gave voice to my own terror and at the same time intensified it. When we came in winter, the snow made the trip even slower and scarier, and my father would have to keep stopping the car to dig a way through a drift or arrange some brush on which we could get over a spot we had skidded on.

But eventually, to my great comfort and joy, we did get to my grandparents' place, in a clearing on a small plateau that held the barn and its yard and the silo; these were the first things you saw, normal and reassuring, when you emerged from the woods. To your right as you came around a curve were the pigpen and the chicken-house (with a tree stump conveniently left there to cut the chickens' heads off on), to your left the dairy sheds where milkcans were washed and stored and the cream separated. As you came around a little further, the road frittered out into what in a French chateau would be called the courtyard; here it was called "out in front," an expanse of rutted dirt with the big drinking trough for the animals, made of algae-covered wood, on one side, and the house rearing up on the other.

Above and behind the house, beyond a small vegetable garden and a line of gooseberry bushes, over the hummocky hillside stretched the pasture, separated from the neighbors' pastures by old stone walls and given character by irregular granite boulders of all sizes with narrow footpaths, bovine and human, winding their way around them. (These boulders, left behind by the glacier as it melted northward, made our major outdoor play equipment, serving all purposes from ponies to dining tables to ladders to slides to hiding-places, and absolutely wonderful to fall off of or scrape your leg on.)

The top of the hill retained a heavy growth of hemlocks, dark and forbidding, and large patches of the same original forest were scattered all over the hill, with maple and beech and birch increasing in the lower reaches. We never went near these woods—they were visibly inhabited by bad things.

The house was built right onto the side of the hill, with high foundations all around; on its lower side, the outhouse (which was connected to the main house) hung out over the abyss in such a way as to provide maximum storage for what are now called solid wastes. I think there must have been a fence of sorts around this area, but it was certainly open to the sky and provided, as its aroma mingled with those of the barn and pigpen, an incomparable richness of atmosphere. (I really perceived it as a richness in my earliest years, not having yet learned to call it nasty.) Below this latrine lived the pigs and chickens whose flesh formed a regular part of our diet, and another hundred feet or so down the hill was the spring from which our water came. The modern mind—too knowledgeable for its own comfort—reels at the potential for disease in these arrangements; I have, in later years, sometimes wondered at the survival of that little community against such biologic odds. But I don't remember ever hearing about outbreaks of typhoid or dysentery; all the digestive tracts I knew of were iron-hardy and it would seem that if they were infected they had gotten quite used to it.

The house, of unpainted wood inside and out, had a generally ramshackle uncared-for look. In the front, a high porch—without a railing—ran the whole length of the building, at least six feet off the ground even at its upper end, where you went up a little abrupt unprotected flight of steps to get to the door. In summer the door was left open, and narrow strips of newspaper were tacked over it to keep the flies out (this did not work).

But as you achieved the porch and paused to get your breath and your bearings, turning away toward the east you were taken by the throat and flung into another sphere of existence. Ten miles away across the valley, crowning and dominating the long skyline of the Green Mountain Range, there rose like a divine word the asymmetrical profile of the mountain known as Camel's Hump. This mountain—only a little over four thousand feet high, but at that the third-highest in the state—is one of those presences with a natural authority over the human spirit. People up there, rough farmers all, speak of it in a special tone of voice, as if it might hear; they glance up at it quickly in the midst of their chores, to call it to witness or to ground themselves in its strength (or of course, sometimes—being farmers—just to see what the weather is up to). I saw it, from the first, as belonging to my family, and myself as belonging to it, forever.

The interior of the house was almost equally remote from my everyday small-town experience, which seemed altogether prosaic and dull by comparison. For me the Hulett home was full of romance, mystery, and the glamor of a bygone time, a sort of hologram surviving out of a previous century. I felt privileged and exhilarated to be admitted into its life; and with equal force I felt that I myself was somehow rooted in this life, that I was growing as it were right out of it, with ties of family going back and back.

The depth and intensity of my feeling for Shaker Hill can be partly accounted for by my having been exposed to it at a very early age, and under special conditions. My first extended visit there lasted probably three or four weeks; I was about three years old; my sister Frances, two years older, was there but not my parents. (The reason for this long visit was that my mother was hospitalized for a thyroid operation and was slow in getting back on her feet.) The whole place and all its inhabitants made the deepest impression on my vulnerable little brain, from which I never fully recovered—an impression that was amplified and embellished in a number of long visits later in my childhood.

You came in, off the porch, directly into the kitchen, where the community life of the house took place: a long narrow dark room laid out with the most exquisite clarity and meaningfulness—or, to a different mind-set, the barest poverty. The darkness never struck me as oppressive; I thought of this room as being all that was homelike and cavelike and majestic; considerations of illumination were as irrelevant as considerations having to do with angels on heads of pins. There was no rug on the floor; the boards were wide, dark, uneven, and rough. Down the left side of the room extended the table, of dark unfinished pine; in my grandmother's day no cloth was used. On the table stood, more or less constantly, a large kerosene lamp, and a wooden trencher that held spoons, and a red cut-glass dish in the shape of a hen that held sugar, and a variety of sturdy heavy ledgers that presumably held records and accounts. Eight or ten plain wooden chairs stood around the table and were pulled out as needed for writing or sewing or peeling potatoes; my grandfather's chair, at the head of the table, was of the kind called a "captain's chair," made all by hand, without nails.

On the left-hand wall hung—mirabile dictu! as my mother would say—a telephone, the kind that lived in a wooden box with two round brass bells in its upper part like two goggling eyes. You stood up, at full attention, to speak into this telephone; children in fact had to stand on a chair. When you wanted to make a call you gave several vigorous cranks to a little handle on the right; this got the attention of the operator, who said "Number please," and then you gave her the number, only one or two digits at that time. In my middle childhood, when I came a few times with my sister and her friend, listening to the nearly constant gossip on the party line was a favorite afternoon recreation. I don't recall that we were ever told this was wrong or an invasion of anyone's privacy, but if any grownup caught us they'd say, "Put that up"; and we did.

Balancing the table to the right was the stove: large, black, wood-burning of course, with a capacious oven and a reservoir (we said "reservore") off to one side holding several gallons of water that gradually heated up as the stove was used; this was the only hot water for the household other than what could be heated in the big iron kettle. The stove had, also, a large black chimney that went up and...out...I suppose. (I have never had an eye for the mechanics of things.) Behind it were usually several pairs of men's boots drying and smelling.

The whole kitchen in fact smelled pretty thrillingly of a vital mixture of smoke, hay and seed, manure, rotting wood, human sweat and greasy food. Down toward the back the outdoor smells abated slightly and the human-sweat-and-greasy-food elements predominated, because this was the area inhabited by the sink. You must not imagine, when I say "sink," a little porcelain confection with a decorative mounting; the sink, like everything else in that house, was a very monster of massive and unadorned functionality. It was made of unpainted and unfinished cast iron, it measured (I don't think I exaggerate) about five feet by two feet by about eight inches deep, it sat three feet off the floor and had a hole at one end through which waste water ran out. Water did not, however, run in; this house did not have running water. Any cold water you needed, you got by dipping it out of an enormous wooden barrel that sat up at the far end of the sink with a tin dipper floating on top; if you needed hot water, you either went to the stove and dipped it out of the reservoir, or if you needed it really hot you boiled some in the kettle (this was not called a "tea" kettle) and poured it directly into your basin.

I don't know how water got into that high barrel. I suppose the water from the spring must have been somehow made to move against gravity; but whether this was done with a pipeline and a pump, or whether the men brought up pailfuls by hand at the crack of dawn, I never wondered about at the time and have no idea today.

At the sink, thirst was assuaged (by drinking directly out of the dipper—the taste was metallic and somewhat rusty); vegetables were washed and scraped and cut up; the kettle was filled; minor ablutions were carried out by the whole family; and of course dishwashing was done.

Dishwashing, in all the country houses I knew in those years—they all had the same terrible black iron sinks—was a perfectly dismal chore involving two large tin pans full of scalding-hot water and some highly inadequate homemade yellow soap that refused to suds, producing instead a yellowish scum that clung to the rim of the pan and thickened as the dishwashing proceeded. Getting the dishes clean was largely a function of "elbow grease," a much-valued cleaning agent throughout my childhood; for really tough burned-on food you could use sand from the yard (since most of the cooking dishes were of cast iron, the sand did them no harm), but much of the residue simply remained, consolidating over time into a uniform black tarry coating. Good housewives, of whom my mother aspired to be one, made a brave show of tackling this revolting job three times a day with vigor and enthusiasm, scrubbing the dishcloth briskly and often over the cake of soap to encourage just a little sudsing, and doing their best to appear womanly and competent in handling the impossible assignment. (It was impossible because there was no way, with that equipment, that you could get the dishes *clean*; it put a terrible strain on the mind's ability to deceive itself.) To make up for the deficiencies in the washing procedure, women often used actively boiling water to rinse—but nothing seemed to touch the greasy tinny rusty smell that permeated the kitchen and everything that was prepared in it.

My father, who was in some ways a wonderful husband, made it his lifelong pride to wipe the dishes after every meal he partook of, and his defense against the depression thus self-imposed was to sing, rather loudly and with forced cheer, the whole time. Fortunately he had a lovely voice, and I learned quite a lot of songs this way. It wasn't so bad, doing the dishes with him wiping. (Besides, people used to say, "Wash and wipe together, live in peace forever"; that seemed to me a goal worth a good deal of drudgery.)

Young children—poor defenseless mites that they are—will believe anything you tell them; they will soak up, and accept as right and good, whatever attitudes and platitudes their culture hands out to them in support of its own peculiarities. So it was with regard to the dishes. I was into my thirties before it even occurred to me that it might be a desirable thing, and not necessarily wicked, to get dishes cleaner with less effort if this was possible. My mind was so deeply imbued with the image of Good Wife, Good Mother, Good Parent, sweating grimly but with conscious virtue over the steaming, unsavory dishpans of my extreme youth that that seemed to me the only correct, the only sanctioned way to wash dishes. And in all honesty I confess that the image still holds its power for me, and that any other approach to dishwashing somehow, in my view, misses the point.

A similar mechanism has worked on me in relation to other domestic chores, done the hard way by my mother out of pure necessity; to this day I have a certain inner resistance to doing them the easy way. "The virtue is in the exertion—in the striving—not in the result," the rubric out of my childhood mutters gravely into my ear;

"only an inferior person lets the detergent (or the machine) (or even gravity) do the work." My intelligence grasps the fallacy of such a view quite clearly, and is entirely willing to be flexible on the point; but my character says nay. (I can even understand, intellectually, that it is not really my character saying nay, but an accidental association of hot greasy water with my childhood feelings about my mother. It feels like my character, though; it feels like a moral issue.)

I digress; that is because this matter of the dishes has something temptingly transcendental about it.

Shaving was not done at the sink. There was a mirror attached to the partition that separated the far-left of the kitchen (containing the pantry) from the far-right (containing the sink). It was fastened quite high and hung at a condescending slant so that even the taller men had to tilt their heads back to get a good look at their faces. Shaving was not, in fact, done very frequently by these farmers (I speak of my grandfather, my Uncle Dennis, and the occasional hired man) and it was an operation to behold, really brightening up the day of any lucky youngster who happened to be around. I think I got the same sense of incipient joy, from finding out that Grandpa was about to shave, that today's preschoolers do from finding out that Sesame Street is on.

First the kettle had to be brought to a boil, and the towel (made from a flour sack) was draped over the right shoulder. Then the long curved steel razor was taken out of its sheath and stropped long and lovingly, with sighs and grunts, on a leather razor strop (the thing that bad children used to get "taken to them," but not in our family). Then the communal shaving mug was taken down from the shelf under the mirror, with its soap and brush sitting in it (I don't know what kind of soap it was, but I'm sure it didn't come from a drugstore; I doubt very much that Starksboro *had* a drugstore). A little hot water was poured in, with all the nicety of judgment involved in making a just-right martini, and the brush was then stirred round and round until a head of good solid suds was worked up. The suds were transferred to the area to be shaved, with many a twirl and twist of the wrist (and, very occasionally, a little dab on the nose of the enraptured watching child if the shaver was feeling communicative); then the razor—which was thoroughly up to its job even if the soap wasn't—was applied, to the accompaniment of more sighs and breath-holdings and, rarely, a "Gol-ding-it" when it cut more than was intended. (I think my male relatives may have used the word "damn" among themselves, but they would certainly never have dreamed of letting a little girl or even a grown woman hear them do so. Those were Puritan days.) Finally shaver and equipment went back to the sink and everything, including the face, got rinsed in cold water, and the now bright red and nearly flayed face got thoroughly abraded with the coarse damp towel (the libretto here expanded into a series of gasps, snorts, and blowings that eventually culminated in a long-drawn-out and satisfied "Aah-h-h"). And that was it for a couple of weeks; and that was as much eloquence and self-expression as I ever heard from any man on those premises.

Baths were another relatively rare undertaking, not performed at the sink. I don't know how the grownups did it (those really were Puritan days), but for children the procedure necessitated heating up the kettle as well as having a reservoir full of reasonably hot water. A large tub of galvanized tin was brought out and placed in front of the stove, whose oven door was open and maintained a continuous blast of hot air; water was poured in to a depth of five or six inches and adjusted to the requisite temperature; the child got in and huddled up, and was washed and lifted out and dried; then the tub was emptied off the edge of the porch. This was not of course done daily, nor yet every other day; even in houses with proper bathtubs, once a week was the norm at that time, for all ages. If there was more than one child in a family the one shallow tub of water did for all, younger before older and girls before boys.

The pantry, as I said, constituted the left-hand side of the far end of the kitchen, separated by a doorway but no door. The pantry smelled of grease and yeast, an excellent smell if you are very hungry, otherwise not. There was also a pervasive smell of mold. Very likely I wasn't allowed in there as a child; I have no clear memories of what went on there, though it must have been a busy place. I assume that's where dough was kneaded, and pies put together, and biscuits made; I know there were shelves, and the dishes (heavy, white, with a brown flowery pattern) were kept there, and any leftover food.

There was no provision, in the immediate vicinity of the kitchen, for keeping food cold; nor am I aware of any cellar to the house where it might have been cooler. Butter was kept, packed in bulk into maple-sugar cans, on a submerged wooden shelf down in the spring; we children were sometimes sent to get it, and I remember how shockingly cold and unbelievably clear that water was; it was too cold even to drink with any comfort, for mouths not used to ice-water.

There was one rocking chair in the kitchen, near the stove and partly behind it. I can remember various men sitting in it mending harness, and whittling, and peeling apples, and rubbing their knees. The women, during the hours when I was up anyway, did their work standing, or used one of the chairs at the big table.

I have no recollection of the members of this household ever talking to each other, at least not in the way of anything you could call conversation. Socially, it was a dead loss. People got on with their work and kept their thoughts to themselves; there seemed to be no concept of giving or receiving pleasure and no expectation of enjoyment from any source (except for my grandfather's rare, quiet, rather malicious chuckling to himself). This was incomprehensible to me, on the part of dwellers in such a fascinating environment; I couldn't understand why they weren't as delighted by it as I was. But of course I respected their emotional privacy, as they mine. People did not pry into other people's minds, up there.

If you turned right immediately on coming into the kitchen, and went through the hall and past the foot of the stairs, you came into the front room. (The term "living room" did not enter my vocabulary until many years later.) I don't know when or whether this room was ever used; it never was during my visits, except by me. I found it a fine room and I was out of the way so nobody minded.

The floor had a linoleum rug on it. Against the left-hand wall stood a largish homemade desk, the kind with a slanting top that you stand erect to work at. Maybe my grandfather worked here at night; I never saw him do so. In the far right corner was a foot-pumped organ. The padded stool on which you sat was made of gingerbreaded oak like the organ itself, and was covered with worn red velvet; there was more red velvet, rather tattered, glued insecurely behind the gingerbread of the organ's face, as a dustcatcher. I spent many fascinated hours with that thing, the first musical instrument of my experience, trying to pick out tunes and experimenting with the various stops that modified the sound produced. I particularly liked the "vox humana" stop, that had an unearthly vibrato to it. My mother must have told me what "vox humana" meant because I seem always to have known it; but the image in my mind was never of a human singer but of some kind of angel choir, not altogether benevolent either. There was no sheet music, not so much as a hymnbook, and I never heard anyone play this organ.

In the middle of the room was a round oak table with a crocheted cloth over it and one or two straight wooden chairs nearby. On the table lay a very large Bible, a real old family Bible with significant events carefully noted in the front, in different handwritings and different shades of brown ink. I remember such names as "Hanner" and "Sarrer," which I thought were pretty quaint (my mother also contributed "Lener" and "Eller" when she wrote up a family history late in her life). Also on this table was a stereoscope, with a dozen or so cards showing the Grand Canal in Venice (at least in retrospect I suppose it was something like that), and simpering pretty girls circa 1895, and romantic rocky chasms, and a squirrel. I looked at those a lot too, and entered into their worlds with the self-abandonment of the very young.

It did not strike me as strange that I never saw the organ played or the desk used or the stereoscope looked at, or anyone but me inhabiting the front room. The very fact of the family's being in possession of these wonderful accouterments was awesome and shed the light of a larger life over the entire household. I knew no other people who owned such things; to me they were riches, and somehow woven through the existence of the farm family like so many threads of gold. (The Biblical and Dickensian references that dropped from my grandfather's lips were similar in implying, to my mind, a vast tapestry of cultural background, not otherwise noticeable in everyday life.)

The remaining rooms on this floor were not part of the house proper, but attached to it in the back. You went out of the kitchen at the far end, and proceeded over a largish platform all of unfinished wood, where vast amounts of stovewood were stored. The floor was incompletely covered with boards; you could look down and see the side of the hill under you, and to me, who never had any sense of balance worth speaking of, it seemed a very dangerous traverse indeed, though it probably was perfectly safe in reality. This transitional room held an overwhelming smell of wood in all stages of freshness and rot, with superadded themes of both sawdust and ordinary dust. But underlying all this was a powerful additional smell which foreshadowed the place you were on your way to.

I forget what this room was called. Certainly not the bathroom; not the outhouse or the toilet or any of the nicknames that more prudish communities give to their useful-places. Most likely it was referred to simply as "out back," in the same way that all sexual parts both male and female were called, by us children at least, and by our parents in our presence, "down there."

Everyone, even today, has some experience of outhouses; but this one was unusual. As the hill fell away very sharply under the house, the place where you sat was a good fifteen feet above ground level, and you could see all the way down, through the floor as well as through the holes (three large and one small) cut into the seat and covered by a single rough spider-infested board when not in use. No lime or other chemicals were used in this contraption. The smell was overpowering, but I was young enough to take it as the natural smell it was; it never bothered me (quite unlike the metallic smells and tastes in the kitchen, which bothered me a whole lot). An old Sears catalogue lay on the floor, serving as interim entertainment and, later, as toilet paper.

I don't know why there were four holes. Certainly as children we went out back together, but I can't imagine the grownups doing so. I merely report the fact.

There was an upstairs to this house, of which we girls only had entree to one room. You went up the dark and enclosed stairs, Grandma preceding you with a candle, and off a similarly dark and unfinished hall you came into a good-sized bedroom containing as its sole piece of furniture (as far as I recall) a perfectly enormous bed, with a perfectly enormous feather mattress on it, whose upper surface lay at least three feet off the ground. There was a trundle bed too, that came out from under the bed; but we didn't use that unless we had other friends with us.

The feather bed was plenty big enough for two little girls; and it was one of the high points of our days to climb up the little wooden stairs on the side of the bed and cast ourselves at full length onto, or rather into, that deliciously accommodating and embracing surface. The sheets were made of old flour sacks sewn together and the quilts were ancient patchwork, not the artistic patchwork one sees in museums but everyday, strictly utilitarian patchwork. But I remember that bed as being the most extravagantly luxurious that ever fell to my lot.

Not that I slept all that well in it. Grandma took the candle away with her when she went downstairs (after a story or two concerning local events that, according to my sister, invariably ended with the phrase "And so—she died") and it was pretty dark up there; and there were two kind of noises, which established themselves forever in my brain as the essence of loneliness and grief. One was the cawing of crows over the hillside that extended below us, which seemed to go on and on during my falling-asleep time; and the other was the eerie hum, something between a sigh and a song, of the wind in the telephone wires strung out across the fields. These sounds, twining and mingling, created a whole population of vividly perceived and fully empathized unhappy beings in my imagination; they still bring a chill to my heart, and a bottomless sorrow. Of course I was legitimately homesick just at that time of day too, which didn't help.

Outdoors there were always wonderful things to do. There was endless fascination in watching the pigs being fed, simply taking in their enormous size and supernaturally deep grunts and ugly faces with white-lashed eyes projecting a malignant intelligence. Watching anything being fed was for that matter full of interest; I suppose there is a kind of fellow-feeling, for a child, in seeing some other creature get his own. Chickens, horses, cows and—especially—calves seemed to have such wonderful appetites, seemed to relish their food so unreservedly. And the men were so generous with the food, big buckets full of it, an orgy every day. The whole place was, I thought, a veritable Paradise for animals, waited on hand and foot, everything done for them. I never, in fact, saw any animals hurt or teased; only, to get them to move or lie down or whatever they were supposed to do, the men would slap them in a comradely way, keeping up a rough kind of one-sided conversation in a special animal language that I didn't understand.

(I did understand about cows being called "Bossy" or "Boss"; but it was not until fifty years later that a suspicion suddenly dawned in my brain and was confirmed by the Oxford Unabridged Dictionary: the origin of this "Boss" is none other than the Romans' "bos, bovis." My grandfather on that remote hilltop in Vermont was speaking a Latin word handed down by plain men, unchanged, through at least three millennia and across half the globe! My roots went deeper than I had imagined.)

It was wonderful watching the cows coming home in the afternoon; I attributed all kinds of sentimental domestic emotions to them which, currently, I consider unlikely. In fact it was not unusual for several of them to fail to come home at milking time at all, so that one of the men had to go out on horseback and get them. On two or three occasions I was given the high honor and almost insupportable happiness of being taken along on this errand, sitting in front of my uncle with his strong arm around me (there was nothing for me to hold on to; we rode bareback) as the horse picked his way along the bumpy hillside and neatly avoided the stones and cowpats. No conversation would be exchanged on these outings; my uncle was, even out of the house, a taciturn man. I never considered him in any way ill-tempered; but he didn't speak unless he had something to say, and even then his mouth opened so very slightly and his utterances were so very terse that I hardly understood a word. Still he somehow inspired confidence, being tall and well-built, and he was a completely gentle person—as in fact were all the people I was lucky enough to grow up among.

I liked watching the cows milling around in the barnyard with their knowledgeable, quiet eyes and their housewifely air. I was fascinated by the cud process; and indeed, having no pets at home and no other opportunities to see large animals on their own turf so to speak, I was deeply interested in *all* the physiological processes so freely indulged in for my edification; they were comparable, I could see, to my own in many ways and yet—so gargantuan in scope! so nobly unselfconscious in execution! like gods! I loved the way they could twitch their ears or make their tails flick up to just the right spot to chase off a fly; I loved the way their hair grew from a neat center in their foreheads, and their knobby but delicate legs.

One breezy day, four or five calves were disporting themselves in the barnyard while the cows were gone. A double sheet of newspaper had been blown into the yard with them, and one calf galloped bravely after it and got its corner firmly into his mouth. The long loose end then flapped and crackled in the wind, back and forth across his face, and scared the poor creature nearly out of his wits; he bucked and tried to back away, twisted from side to side and rolled his eyes frantically, never realizing that he was holding this monster himself and had only to open his mouth to get rid of it. My sister and I thought he was having fun with the paper, and were delighted with the show; calves were rarely so lively. So we ran to the house for more newspaper and were enthusiastically throwing it into the barnyard for the other calves when some grownup saw what we were up to, took the paper away from us and from the poor bedevilled animal, and said, without emphasis, "Don't do that. Scares him."

Watching the milking was wonderful: warm and swish-swish-swish into the pail, and how delicious it was to drink, just like that, out of a tin cup! Watching the horses get harnessed was wonderful: enormous dark-brown creatures, strong and patient, with a smell different from that of the cows but just as authentic, understanding just as the cows did what the men meant by their ceaseless mutterings and their guiding hands; they bent their necks and raised their feet so obediently, it was like a dance between man and animal. The harness itself, old cracked black leather with brass fittings almost equally black, was beautiful to me; so solid, so experienced, so exactly right for its purpose, so purposefully and comfortably creaking as it took its place around the horse's belly or under his chin. I loved to see the horses drink at the trough with all their harness on. I marvelled how they could swallow with the big iron bits in their mouths, and in fact they were not too neat about it; when they raised their heads beards of green algae hung down, on which they would chomp complacently.

I was intrigued by the mysteries of the dairy shed too, but "younguns" were not encouraged to hang around there, and the machinery noises and gleam of bright clean metal were intimidating anyhow; it didn't seem like a children's kind of place. Back to the barn, in through the wide entrance where the haymow was, and behind it the loft with hay almost up to the ceiling. This was probably our most frequent play-place, offering ideal opportunities for just resting or sulking; hide and seek; bury-your-sister; or, best of all, jumping from the top of the hayloft down onto the thick lower level of the mow. This was a leap of a good six or eight feet, and it took me a while to get up my nerve; finally, when some neighbor boys came over to play one day, I got into the spirit of the thing through a combination of mob psychology and bullying, and became, for that one season, quite an addict.

A couple of summers we happened to be on the farm during haying. I was probably nine or ten then, and was completely entranced with this process, carried out still in the old-fashioned way, the hay being scythed down by hand, gathered (with a pitchfork) into neat piles about a yard in each dimension, and the piles individually hoisted (again, by pitchfork, with incredible strength and grace and precision) to the top of the hay wagon, where one or two men fitted each forkful into the beautifully balanced load until it was about eight feet high. Any spectators who were around when the wagon was fully loaded could be, on request, lifted up to the top with all the men and take part in the careful but still bumpy progress back to the barn, where the hay was unloaded in the same perfectly constructed piles.

Of course this was in the heat of early summer, and at that time (at least, on that farm) grown men did not take off half their clothes

just because they were warm; they remained decently dressed in
long-sleeved, fully-buttoned-up shirts of coarse printed cotton, and
heavy denim "overhalls," as well as battered straw hats. (A few years
later, my uncle had a severe bout of asthma and stayed, in bed, in
our house in Bennington while his case was being worked up. I remember being dumbfounded at seeing the skin of his arms and
torso, fair and unspotted as a nun's; I had assumed unconsciously
that the coarse red crosshatched skin of his face was his natural en-
dowment, and the same all over.)

In the middle of the mornings and again in the middle of the afternoons we girls would be sent out from the house to the hayfield
with maple-sugar cans full of "drink"—a mixture of vinegar, sugar
and water—and the tin dipper; we would move around among the
lordly creatures at work, most of whom were hired just for the
haying and not known to us by name, and timidly offer a full dipper,
about a pint, to each in turn. Each man would take two drinks, and
signify his repletion and thanks with a quick nod, which was neither
intended nor perceived as being deficient in courtesy; it was the accepted way, up there, of saying "Thank you very much." Smiles were
not used.

People did speak differently on Shaker Hill. It was, after all, a
cul-de-sac within a cul-de-sac, minimally connected to the rest of the
world since its very beginnings, which were most likely in the late
eighteenth century (General John Stark, for whom the town was
named, was a Vermont hero of the Revolution, nearly as highly
thought of locally as Ethan Allen himself). In this isolated and in-
bred community, the spoken language retained definite ghosts of an
older form of English. "Hain't" for "ain't," "coomb" for "comb," "et"
for "ate," "vittles" for "food," "nawthin" for "nothing," "yourn" for
"yours" were normal words here, along with strange constructions
and usages: "Be ye goin' to taown this forenoon?" My mother continued to use "forenoon," meaning "morning," all her life, though
she dropped most of the rest of it.

The most striking feature of the speech, aside from its grudging
overall quantity, was this "aow" sound, used wherever most Ameri-
cans would say "ow"; as far as I know it was unique to rural com-

munities in northern Vermont. The short a's were pronounced very flat, even in words like can't and aunt and laugh; the r's were almost savagely clear. This was nothing like the Maine and New Hampshire and Massachusetts accents, all of which had softer r's and none of which had the "aow" vowel (though Maine shares with Vermont, still, the affirmative word "Ayuh," ending in a glottal stop). This special way of talking added still further to the prestige of Shaker Hill for my young mind.

The regular inhabitants of the house, when I was little, were my grandparents and their two sons: Dennis, who must have been about thirty, and Kenneth, who was still a teenager and not much in evidence. A second daughter, Ruth (pronounced Rewth), had like my mother gotten away, by marrying the Starksboro blacksmith.

My grandfather, Frank Hulett, had a long Yankee face with surprisingly bright red cheeks and lips shining out of a pepper-and-salt beard that he normally kept closely trimmed and for some periods shaved off altogether. For a long time he was the only man I knew with a beard and I identified him quite strongly with Santa Claus. His eyes were bright blue and twinkled; he often seemed to be nursing a private joke. As I got older, I realized that most of his amusement came from the stupidity and failings of others and his own ability to get the best of them. He liked to tell stories on these themes, when he visited us in Bennington; when he got to the point of his victim's final discomfiture and rout, he would hug his elbows and shake with silent laughter, his cheeks screwed up tight and red and his eyes twinkling madly.

Grandpa was a smart man, I always thought, though with little schooling; when he died he left a significant nest egg in a Burlington bank, bearing witness to his "shrewdness and thrift." He was at one time, I believe, selectman in Starksboro: an elected position of some dignity and responsibility. And he had the further distinction (in my mind) of being able to remember hearing, as a young boy, the news of Lincoln's assassination. Except for these modest claims to fame, though, he was a small dairy farmer all his life, with a herd of about twenty cows. As far as I am aware, he never saw the inside of a church; still, there was that big Bible in his living room, and there were Old-Testament overtones to a good deal of his conversation, references to the Queen of Sheba and the Witch of Endor and the hosts of Midian, thrown out so casually that I had the vague impression he had known them all personally. Maybe he *was* a Bible-reader, or maybe these references had just come down to him through his own parents, I don't know.

He had apparently read *David Copperfield* at one time; he used to say he'd gone to school with Uriah Heep. And a phrase commonly used by both him and my mother to indicate willingness to go along with a proposed scheme was "Barkis is willin'"; I of course picked it up and used it too, though it was some years before I came across the original and understood its context.

I have, still, several vivid mental pictures of my grandfather: 1. Trimming his beard, or sometimes shaving, in front of the looking glass in the kitchen. 2. Milking cows, squatting on a three-legged stool and grimacing with the effort. At first I thought he was smiling, but he wasn't. 3. Playing checkers with me. This was not a social game but a strict contest of the mind, in which he pulled no punches (I was six or seven when these games began) and invariably won. In the middle of the game, when he had got me in a trap, he would lean back in his chair grinning and say: "*Na-a-ow,* Mr. John Henry Braown, what you goin' to dew when the rent comes raoun?" He was always willing to play, if he had time, but he always won. 4. Peeling an apple, an activity for which he was renowned in the family. He did it with his jackknife, and the peel came off unbelievably thin, almost transparent, in one long curl. He then cut the apple up and handed it around, one slice at a time, on his knife blade; the pieces tasted a little of rust.

I liked and admired my grandfather greatly and tried to cultivate his company, but he had no real use for younguns and didn't seem to notice.

My grandmother Emma was a subordinate person in the household, which was manifestly run by and for the benefit of the men. This was less a matter of habitual sexual attitudes than of the capacities of the individuals involved. Emma was Frank's second wife, the first (her sister) having died shortly after their marriage and having begged Frank on her deathbed to "take care of Emma"; she was the mother of the four children. I came to realize, by the time I was grown up, that she was what educators nowadays call limited, and really required "taking care of"; she could read, barely, but was not able to buy things in a store (she did not know how to make change) or to come to even simple domestic decisions. Unfortunately she did not have the sweetness of disposition that often goes with mental inferiority; she was a nosy, interfering, cantankerous, hidebound and ignorant woman.

Later on Grandma lived alternately with her two daughters for many years, quite a thorn in their respective sides but one that neither ever complained about (Yankees did not complain, they just tightened their lips and did their duty). But at the time I am speaking of she was still taking care, in her way, of the house on Shaker Hill and cooking for the three men, as well as for the hired men who came for haying and potato-digging and so on. She had about the status of a hired girl herself.

My grandparents separated when I was in my early teens, and my Uncle Dennis took over the farm. He married a nice girl named Mary and they had two little daughters; once, in my middle teens, I visited them. It was a terrible disappointment. Everything had changed: linoleum lay on the floor, starched ruffled curtains hung at the windows, electric light shone in every room; there were even pictures on the walls. It seemed pretty decadent to me. Then my uncle's asthma got very bad and was found to be due to wheat; he moved his family to Bristol and worked in a dairy there. Our two families barely kept in touch.

The years went by, as they do. When I was over sixty years old, and in that part of the state for another reason, I made a detour with my husband and daughter to see Shaker Hill again. The road up the hill hadn't changed much but our strong new car took it in high gear all the way. The house had been bought by a religious community and turned into a retreat; the barn and silo, the dairy shed, the pig pen and chicken yard and drinking trough were all gone. Where the barnyard used to be was a charming rock garden, shaded by an enormous old butternut tree whose trunk, in my childhood, had been only as thick as a man's arm. We found the spring down on the hillside, protected with a little wooden roof and apparently still in some kind of use.

We didn't go in the house.

Pitkins

A CROW, STARTING FROM SHAKER HILL—say one of those that used to haunt my bedtime—flying east and just a little north over the ridge of the Green Mountains, past Montpelier the state capital and on along the wide Winooski River valley nearly to its source, would come in a total of thirty-five miles or so to another small farming community called Marshfield. This gentle place was settled in the winter of 1794 by one Caleb Pitkin, his brand-new wife Hannah, and two other young couples; they pulled their belongings by hand sled over four feet of snow the whole fifteen miles from Montpelier because there was no road and they had no horses. The town has been a veritable nest of Pitkins ever since.

Caleb and all his descendants were living presences to my father and his brothers; the entire history of the town and its people was a matter of everyday talk among them, something intimately known. As on Shaker Hill, there were relatively few families in Marshfield, intermarried to an astonishing degree; I knew almost none of them personally, but their names—the Dwinells, the Drinkwaters, the Blisses, the Fifields, the Browns—were sprinkled all through the background conversations of my childhood. Anecdotes dating back a hundred years or more were told as if they had happened last week, and were given reality for me by the half-absorbed knowledge that, for example, So-and-so's granddaughter's stepson was in fact my own second cousin.

The sense of family continuity went back even further, before the founding of Marshfield, through more than a century of Connecticut Pitkins prominent in manufacturing and politics, all the way to one William, a lawyer, who came over from England in 1659 to make a name for himself in the New World. The Severance family too, from which my grandmother Pitkin sprang, had been established and prominent in nearby Cabot (where the cheese now comes from) since about 1800, and before that for over a hundred years in New Hampshire; they traced themselves back, in England, as far as the time of Henry VIII.

I didn't know all this until years later, but I understood well enough that a person might take a quiet satisfaction in being a Pitkin; and I was well aware of the corollary, that a certain moral elevation was expected to be manifest as a Pitkin moved through life. I don't recall that anyone ever spoke to me on this kind of subject—it is highly unlikely that anyone would have—but the idea came through all right, that Pitkins were special, and therefore under special obligation.

This was a church-going family, a talking, reading, singing family, and the sense of an ethical and even social tone suffusing it was considerably stronger than in the case of my Starksboro forebears. (The Huletts were in no way *un*ethical, you understand; just... shrewd.) My father once quoted my grandmother Olive as saying, "I have always moved in the best society available to me"; this struck me, in my censorious teens, as both snobbish and a bit high-flown from a backwoods farmer's wife, but I have come to see it differently. As a small child, though, I found my Pitkin grandparents and their home a trifle intimidating, and I think this was partly because of their slightly higher level of civilization. Another reason may have been that we didn't visit them nearly as often as we did my mother's relatives, and were never left there alone, to bond with the place on our own. In Marshfield, with parents present, there was always a social role to play, and expectations to fulfill; in Starksboro, a child was just one more critter to be fed, nobody cared if you disappeared for a while or got dirty, and what went on in your head was your own business—a much more comfortable state of affairs for a youngster as shy and self-conscious as I.

In any case, and for whatever reason, my memories of the Marshfield farm are far blurrier than those of Shaker Hill. It was distinguished by having a name ("The Pines"), and stood just off the main road between Marshfield and Cabot. My grandfather had been a self-taught surveyor and civil engineer for some years and had even lived for a while in South Dakota where—of all places—my own father, Paul, was born; but by the time I came along he (my grandfather) had settled to a quiet farming life again, having, like Grandpa Hulett, a small herd of cows and a big hayfield. The house and outbuildings were thus categorically quite similar to the Hulett place; only everything was "nicer," cleaner, better-kept. In the Pines parlor there were comfortable cushions on the heavy oak chairs, protected by crocheted antimacassars; people came and sat and read books and did their mending there rather than in the kitchen; the organ was in regular use and there was sheet music as well as hymnbooks on its rack; enlarged and tinted photographs of the children, in thick oval gilt frames, hung on the walls; the big kitchen stove was kept smooth and shiny by regular blacking; and the pillowcases on the beds upstairs had flower sprays hand-embroidered on them.

Some of these differences may have been due to a better financial status—or greater willingness to spend—but I think the main factor was the energy and spirit of my Grandmother Pitkin. When she was a young girl in the seventies she had had the nickname of "Powder"; I assumed as a child that this had to do with her using face-powder, but was told much later on that it was short for Gunpowder, and referred to her forceful nature. (Genetic note: my sister Frances, who had many of Grandma Pitkin's qualities, was known as "Bang" all through her teens.) Grandma had been a church organist, school teacher, and music teacher from the age of fifteen; married at nineteen; bore eight children, five of whom she raised to extremely competent manhood; was active in the church and community; took care of her own chickens and sold the eggs to pay for "extras" for the house; of course kept her own home and made her own clothes, both very well; and was a particular whiz at making braided rugs.

These braided rugs were a regular *leitmotif* of my childhood. They were all over Grandma's house, and all over our house as well. I was taught to consider this a major talent, and my mother was prone to sigh deeply and say she never could make rugs like Mother Pitkin. They were made, naturally, from old woolen clothes; Grandma always had a sharp eye for a suit or jacket of good color that would go with material she already had, and sometimes, according to my father, couldn't wait until things were decently worn out before cutting them up. My mother also braided, although she felt obliged to deprecate her own efforts; and I myself have been saving old woolens for forty years in order to be a credit to my grandmother. They are overflowing the large cedar chest where I keep them and I am beginning to feel the pressure, never having even learned the technique beyond the rudiments that my mother taught me long ago. This kind of expectation is ground deeply into the tender minds of the young, and strongly resists subsequent modification. I can perfectly well grasp the irrationality of hanging on to it; but in my heart I know that to make a work of art and an heirloom out of those scraps is not only my duty but probably my main duty at this point in my life; and that I will leave something important undone if I don't get to it.

It wasn't just the rugs. My sister and I, and our girl cousins, were taught to admire and revere Grandma Pitkin in every possible way; and did, of course. She was a brisk and chipper lady, moderately buxom, who waddled from side to side as she walked; to me she was a goddess, an unattainable model. She had the remnants of considerable prettiness even in old age; her hair was always agreeably waved around her face; her cotton print dresses, at least the "better" ones, had little white lace collars; even her aprons were trimmed with rickrack, and were always fresh and crisp. Her sons adored her, and it was years before I realized that not only my mother, but all five of the daughters-in-law, could have done very well without Mrs. Standard-of-Comparison in every aspect of their lives. Nobody ever said anything to such a shocking effect, but I got to the point where I understood the meaning of the compressed lip and the averted glance when the subject of Mother Pitkin came into the conversation.

Grandma, in her own house, was all over the place: shaking out her rugs, kneading bread in the big kitchen, feeding her chickens, mopping the floor. She moved around fast. You noticed her; where she was, things were stirred up. Even when she visited us, she would bring along some large work project, a rug to be sewn together or a new dress to be cut out and run up on my mother's foot-treadle Singer. I remember Mother hovering uncertainly in the doorway of our dining room and looking with anxious eyes at Grandma (who stood with shears in her hand and a mouth full of pins), hardly daring to ask when she might put the next meal on the table that had been so cheerfully and high-handedly appropriated.

Grandma had a beautiful smile, and I believe her instincts were perfectly benevolent (all of her sons were unusually sweet-natured men, and I don't think they got it from Grandpa). But they were expressed in such very crisp, self-confident tones that I at least was painfully abashed in her presence, never feeling that I would quite measure up to her standards, and preferring—when I had a choice—to render homage from an inconspicuous distance.

A man married to a woman like that is of necessity a quiet retiring man, otherwise there would be explosions. And my grandfather Pitkin—whose given name was the old family one of Ozias (Oh-*zye*-us)—was, as far as my immature perceptions went, very much in the background, a rather delicate-looking gentlemanly old man with a wispy voice, thick glasses, and a careful step, always wearing a hat in or out of the house, seeming usually to be absorbed in his own thoughts or in what he was reading. Occasionally he would indeed make some sharp remark in contradiction to Grandma, as if to make it clear that he knew perfectly well what was going on and that there were limits beyond which Olive's excesses would simply have to be curbed; then a few sparks would fly back and forth. Nothing serious, just a comfortable accustomed sort of verbal swatting, and then it would die down.

There was one story my father used to tell, though, having to do with the time in his own childhood when Ozias made root beer. In those days—and well into my childhood too—you made your own root beer by putting water and sugar and some vital essence you got at the drug store into bottles and waiting for nature to take its course. You had to test it from time to time to see if nature had taken its course sufficiently yet—that is, if there was enough fizz to give the right punch to the brew. Well, so Ozias made some root beer, and he decided to test out a bottle one day when, as it happened, Olive had just painted her kitchen. The root beer was being aged in the woodshed behind the kitchen, but Ozias brought a bottle inside.

"Ozias," says Olive, says she (Ozias, in a connection such as this, was pronounced with a strong upward inflection on the last syllable), "don't you open that bottle in my kitchen."

"Oh," says Ozias, says he, "I can hold it with my thumb."

Well, he couldn't. And the root beer—which was fully mature—splashed all over the newly-painted kitchen. And I believe Olive did not speak to Ozias again for several weeks.

So maybe there were some explosions, in the early days.

My father and his brothers had, among them, five daughters; not until I was six did a pair of twin boys make their appearance—at which the family breathed a sigh of thanksgiving and knew the name would be carried on. It was about that same time that the Family Reunions began, and in a couple of years settled into an unbreakable pattern.

They were held just outside Marshfield, on an early-nineteenth-century farm once belonging to my grandfather's uncle; it had continued to be called, locally, the Levi Pitkin farm, and in the family was known simply as the Levi. Olive and Ozias, their sons and daughters-in-law, and—after another boy came along—the eight grandchildren made up the core of the gathering, but it was invariably supplemented by my grandmother's sister Sue, three or four cousins of complicated degrees of consanguinity, and occasionally a relation or two of one of the wives. The festivities lasted usually from Saturday afternoon through Sunday evening and included two major outdoor meals on improvised board tables, as well as horseshoe-playing, tractor-riding, ball-throwing, and little skits put on by each family for the benefit of my uncle Fred's movie camera (this was only about 1930; most home photographers were using box Brownies, but my uncle Fred got into home movies from the beginning).

The house was in a neglected state when the Reunions began, still with its outhouse (which my cousins had papered over with pictures of Greta Garbo) and black iron sink and ancient peeling flowered wallpaper. A kerosene stove provided the only cooking facility, and a small Franklin stove warmed up the big dining room on chilly mornings (none of the chimneys in the old fireplaces could yet be induced to draw). We children slept in a large unfurnished space under the roof, giggling, reading under the covers with flashlights, trading riddles and getting into pillow fights as late as our parents would let us (that was usually shortly after they discovered the apple-pie beds we had made for them). By day we roamed the woods and competed in stilt-walking on the lawn (my father had made stilts to suit children of all sizes); we picked wild strawberries for the women to use on shortcake, and made up secret languages. Without specific attention we soaked up the presence of our elders, those multiple wise beings of different ages but mysteriously similar physiognomy and apparently total telepathic agreement on all matters of importance (like when it was time for lunch and whether there would or would not be a swimming expedition in the afternoon and exactly when and under what circumstances Cousin Obadiah had lost his leg in the horse-pulling accident); and forged, year by year, ties of intimate relationship that came to full strength in adolescence and have withstood, undiminished, decades of subsequent neglect.

The Reunions are now in their sixty-eighth year and include nearly ninety participants. Circumstances have kept me away from all but a few since I became an adult, but when I do go I am instantly eight years old and barefoot, and that is my family. At the same time I am aware, as if in a dream, that my hair is almost white and that the other children whose hearts have been so long linked to mine have almost-white hair too. We smile at the little ones playing on the sunlit lawn, and compare stories of "the boys" (our fathers), and of Grandma (whom we all so uncannily resemble), and feel ourselves partaking—unexpectedly, bemusedly—of eternity.

A Love Story

WHEN MY FATHER WAS well into his eighties, living in the Vermont Veterans' Home in Bennington after my mother died, he got unaccustomedly chatty one afternoon and told me for the first time about their courtship.

My mother, it seems, after several years of teaching school in Starksboro, had attended Middlebury College for two years, after which she had to return home. Whether this was for money reasons or whether she was just needed to hold the family together, I don't know. She was a bright and I think an ambitious girl; it must have been like the end of the world for her. My father—who had had, like his brothers, to take his turn helping Grandpa on the farm before starting college and was already in his middle twenties—did not arrive in Middlebury until the year after she left; then he began to hear his fellow students extolling the virtues of one red-headed Fannie Hulett (he was always partial to red hair). He wouldn't tell me exactly what they said—something about her character, he implied. Anyway, he was deeply impressed; so much so that in his second year (having looked around at other girls and found them wanting) he worked up his courage, got her address from the administrative office, and wrote her a respectful letter introducing himself and begging for the honor of her acquaintance. She answered (who wouldn't?); they exchanged photographs; and a steady correspondence ensued, that lasted for more than a year before a meeting was possible. The way this worked out was that my father, after his junior year, joined the Naval Reserve as many of his classmates were doing (America had just entered World War I), and in this connection had to make an appearance in the town of Vergennes, a mere fifteen miles from Starksboro; he would then have nearly a full day to get back to his training camp on Long Island.

"You ask your father if you can take his wagon," he wrote to Fannie, "and you drive along the Vergennes road and look out for a young man in a navy uniform, on the right-hand side of the road, walking toward Starksboro." Which Fannie did. And the meeting came off so successfully (Paul was an unusually handsome young man and Fannie was not so bad herself, a "fine young woman" with a certain salty strength—as well as that wonderful red hair) that later in the summer they got together again, for an afternoon of climbing Camel's Hump with Fannie's sister Ruth and her fiancé the blacksmith.

Shortly after that the war ended. (My father regretted all his life that he never got to see active service, and sixty years later he objected vigorously to being received in the Veterans' Home because he felt he hadn't earned it.) He went back to Middlebury for his last year, and by the time he graduated he and Fannie were engaged. Tentatively engaged, that is; with true Yankee caution, they agreed to spend a year getting to know each other better on an everyday basis. My father got a job in a machine shop in Springfield and found a job for my mother as maid in a house a few blocks away from the one where he boarded; and for a whole year they worked, saved their money, "walked out" in the evenings, and confirmed their intention of marrying. The wedding came about in June 1920. My grandfather Hulett, in the most generous gesture I ever heard of on his part, gave them fifty dollars as a wedding present, and on it they travelled to Boston and stayed there in a hotel for an entire week.

After the honeymoon my father began teaching (like three of his four brothers), and shortly became principal of the high school in MacIndoes Falls; a couple of years later he was named superintendent of schools in West Charleston. But his career in education was flawed, hopelessly as far as he was concerned, by the need to "play politics" with the town; my father had an innocence of mind that could simply not accommodate compromise or stratagem. So in 1926 he decided to be an insurance salesman and moved the little family (my sister Frances was five, I was not quite four) to

Bennington in the southwest corner of the state. We lived in half of a double house on Silver Street in the hilly part of the town until I was nine, and then bought a trim little house, with a porch and a good-sized yard out back, on Warn Street over near the river; there my sister and I got to be adolescents and finally left, and there my parents lived all the rest of their lives and turned into perfectly splendid grandparents.

Now that, you must agree, is a good story, of its own (sadly outmoded) kind. And the marriage, although probably not as perfect as the two young people envisioned it, endured solidly for fifty-two years, until my mother's death did them part. My father in his dotage would say mournfully that there was never a cross word between them; that was not *quite* true, but close enough.

Interlude

BENNINGTON IS WHAT I THINK OF as my hometown. It lies in a hollow near the edge of the Green Mountains (which are hardly ever green; purple is their most constant tone, a beautiful soft, melting and changing purple). Bald Mountain to the north, Woodford to the east, Harmon Hill to the southeast, and Mount Anthony to the southwest, all backed by innumerable others whose names I never knew: these were the beings that watched over my childhood—that were always there—that understood. After I moved away, it took decades of living in flat country for me to accept the reality and security of any place not rimmed by mountains. A town on the prairie—where I *have* lived, unwillingly and briefly—hardly seems, to a mountain person, like a place at all; it has no definition, no location; you have an uneasy feeling that you might fall off; and when you look up in your trouble there is nobody there. In Bennington the mountains hold you safe, and you know you are at home.

So much then for my antecedents; now for my introduction into society.

School

ETWEEN THE AGES OF FIVE AND THIRTEEN we all (the Protestants, that is) attended the Bennington Graded School on School Street, about half a mile from our house. This was a Victorian pile of red brick in a large waste of playground (separated into "boys' side" and "girls' side") with a few indestructible swings, seesaws and slides, and plenty of room for the round games, snap-the-whips and tag that were our mainstays. Parts of the playground lay lower than the rest and in the winter these parts would puddle and freeze over, making wonderful sliding-places. The big kids negotiated them erect but the little ones simply slid on their knees; and one of the saddest memories of my early life is the day I wore holes in this way through a brand-new pair of brown stockings and made my mother cry. It took a lot to make her cry; but I guess it took a lot to achieve a new pair of brown stockings too.

A couple of blocks further along School Street was the Catholic school of St. Francis de Sales, with which we had nothing whatever to do. Bennington had a large French-Canadian population; the Catholic church (St. Peter's) was by far the biggest in town, and St. Francis' school was at least as big as ours. But the children did not mix, unless they happened to live on the same block; I didn't know a single Catholic child by name, and thought of them as a distinctly different race right up to high school. Then we all went to Ben-Hi together and were integrated with perfect smoothness, falling in and out of puppy love across the terrible sectarian gulf with no trouble at all.

(There were only a few Jewish families in Bennington, as well as a few Greeks and Syrians; their children all came to the Graded School and mixed in with the rest of us without notice or incident. Our families didn't deal with each other socially, but the distinction was of the same kind as with the Methodists and Baptists. *Catholics* were something else again.)

Just before you got to our school, the street crossed over the Roaring Branch (its full name is the Roaring Branch of the Walloomsac River; locally, it is known simply as the Branch). During most of the year this fiercely-named brook has about eight inches of water, running quietly along the bottom of a gully fifteen feet wide and maybe ten feet deep, over a bed of roundish granite rocks in all sizes. Only in the spring thaw, when the snow melts suddenly off the mountains to the north and east and comes crashing down through the Branch, does it rise—sometimes even to overflowing—and justify its appellation by tumbling the rocks of its bed over and over like so many marbles, so that the town lives with thunder day and night.

The Branch was in its sedate phase the September when I first started to school and I remember being shown by whoever was taking me—probably just a group of the neighborhood children—how if you stood on the little bridge and gazed over its rails, looking down on the water as it streamed toward you from the north and buried itself under your feet, you got the distinct illusion that you and the whole bridge (your ship) were sailing northward on the surface of the river and heading for—who knows where, some place certainly out of a fairytale, bound on an adventure half thrilling and half terrifying. This became a favorite recreation of mine; I almost always stopped for a couple of minutes on the way to and from school. Some of the kids liked to throw sticks or chips of wood into the water on the east side and then dash across the street, to their own great peril in the traffic, to see them emerge on the west side; but I liked just to stand on the deck, as it were, and feel myself sailing far, far away.

The front entrance to the Graded School was never used in my memory, though once in a while, all through my life, I have had a dream of going up those granite steps, through the heavy doors into the big dark wood-panelled hall, and being greeted by the old smells of oil, sawdust, chalk, and unwashed childhood that meant "school" to me. (The wooden floors had an oil finish which, every evening, was sprinkled with sawdust and swept up by the janitor. Children did not, of course, sit on school floors in those days; floors had germs. Out of school we sat on floors—and even sidewalks—and went barefoot in three seasons of the year; but school had different standards.) We normally came into the building by the two side entrances, with "BOYS" and "GIRLS" carved in their granite lintels as immutably as the Ten Commandments. In waiting to be let in, and in coming up the worn stone steps, and in moving around the halls for any reason at all, we kept a strict single-file formation which was enforced by an ever-present teacher.

The floors were dark, the windows were large but placed high, and many-paned so they didn't admit a lot of light. The days are relatively short in Vermont during the school season and my recollections of every classroom I knew there are shot through with a sense of high-ceilinged darkness inadequately modified by dim yellow light bulbs, and that quite oppressive, totally characteristic smell.

Kindergarten was on the first floor, attended by Miss Gertrude Carney, a sweet-faced low-voiced gray-haired lady. I thought kindergarten was absolutely wonderful. I already knew how to read and write, so the intimations of that particular mystery to be imparted didn't impress me unduly; but the availability of so much crisp virgin paper, and crayons of all colors, and scissors that we were actually encouraged to cut with; and the marvelous blackboards all around the room, with chalks that even the pupils got to use once in a while; and the group-singing of lovely little songs; and the linings-up for every conceivable activity, from visiting the toilets to the monthly inspections by the school nurse; all were to me the delightful perquisites of a greater world than I had so far even suspected, and I was enthralled.

Oh, but those toilets! They were in the basement of the building, and until I reached the yet greater world of high school "going to the basement" was the only expression I knew for indicating, to anyone other than my family, what I had in mind. There was a boys' side and a girls' side and a wall between them, with no door in it. I don't recall that the necessary arrangements were poorly supplied or cared for in any way, but they were lighted (and ventilated) only by tiny high windows; and they smelled and clanged and rusted; and it was cold; and here and there in the dim damp hallway were sinister un-explained little doors and side turnings where something might be; and the stairs themselves exuded a gritty black sweat. The basement almost immediately became one of the looming menacing presences in my dreams, where bad things were always about to happen. I went down there as little as humanly possible.

First grade was pretty dark-haired Miss Hudson, in whose room we learned a new song:

> Good morning to you,
> Good morning to you!
> We're all in our places,
> With sunshiny faces.
> Oh, this is the way
> To start a new day.

This song was taught us by Mrs. Trussell the music teacher, and my life reached new levels of bliss and richness. Mrs. Trussell came into the classroom two or three times a week, wheeling in front of her a little foot-pedalled mini-organ of about three octaves, and taught us to sing and to read music. Quite well, too; we had part-singing from the very first year. She wrote music on the blackboard with the aid of a gadget that held five pieces of chalk at once, so she could lay out a whole staff evenly across the board; I found this amazing.

Even before we sang the song each day, Miss Hudson would say politely, "Good morning, children," and we would say, in unison, "Good morning, Miss Hudson." I remember how this gave me the feeling of having learned something important, how I seemed to have gone through an initiation and become a full member of soci-ety. (What ceremonious creatures children are!) But I didn't get to savor this pleasure for long because once it was verified that I could read and write already (my mother had been a schoolteacher, remember) I was sent on to second grade, with Miss Moore.

Miss Moore was a kind and gentle woman but a real stickler for manners. I don't remember that we went through the "Good morning, children" ritual in her room, nor did we sing "Good morning to you"; instead we all rose, first thing every morning, and recited the Pledge of Allegiance, throwing our little arms out dramatically on the word "flag" toward the very large specimen standing in the corner behind Miss Moore's desk. I learned this Pledge in, I suppose, a reasonable number of weeks, just from hearing it every day; but I distinctly remember how, for some time, it puzzled me. Several of the words were previously unknown to me and I could not get the syllables to carry any meaning to my brain. "I pledge a Legions"—?? "One nation, in the Visible"—what could it possibly refer to? (I was having a similar trouble, at about the same period, in relation to the words of "My Country, 'Tis of Thee," where in the second verse the poet addresses "Our fathers' God…Author of Liberty." The word "author," pronounced by Vermonters with an "ah" sound rather than an "aw," I heard as "Arthur"; and I knew only one Arthur, a very nice pink-cheeked classmate on whom I had a small crush. How he got mixed up in these high liturgical affairs, to the point of having his name in a real song, was a great mystery. It is true, of course, that he was an Episcopalian; that might account for it.)

Anyway it was Miss Moore, for me as for, I suspect, many members of our class, who in the course of a very few months persuaded us that we really should rise when she entered the room, look her in the eye when we spoke to her (as country children we tended to look anywhere *but* at the person to whom we were speaking), and use her name at least once in each communication, like good upper-class servants. "Now how much is two and five?" "Two and five is seven, Miss Moore." "And then if you take away one?" "Take away one is six, Miss Moore." These habits became deeply ingrained, and when one day Georgie Bahan squirmed in his desk to the point of upsetting its balance completely, so that it and he fell to the ground in a tangle, he raised his hand for permission to speak before blurting out, "Oh Miss Moore, Miss Moore, I think I've broken my arm, Miss Moore!" He had, too.

Second grade otherwise consisted, as far as my memories go, in a grand performance of some kind in which I and three other girls, dressed in painstakingly ruffled blue crepe-paper dresses, swayed in synchrony and sang a song about being bluebells in the dell; and learning about the aurora borealis from Mrs. Kenyon the drawing teacher, who had us all making colored pictures of igloos with impossibly brilliant rainbows behind them. (You can really see these northern lights sometimes in Bennington, and it always takes me back to second grade and Miss Moore's class; though the ones in the sky are pretty pallid compared to the ones we drew.)

And then there was the day we had a guest speaker, an evangelistic little lady from the SPCA, who advised us (as I understood it) to go home and put fishhooks in the insides of our cheeks so we would know how it felt to the fish. I retailed this advice to my parents after school, and my father (who dearly loved both hunting and fishing) got as angry as I've ever seen him, and called that poor lady many derogatory Yankee names ("witch" is the only one I remember, but I know there was a sizzling series).

Third grade, Miss Holden. She was old even then, at least we children thought so; and she was the only teacher in my whole experience who went in for corporal punishment, in the shape of a wooden ruler that hung in her supplies closet and that the offending boy would be required to bring to her so she could smack his open palm two or three times. We, as a class, were fortunate at this time in numbering among our members two bona fide Bad Boys, dashing older fellows from the outskirts of town who, as far as I could see, came to school only when they felt like it and seemed likely to spend the rest of their young manhood getting through grade school; so we were treated to the delightfully horrifying spectacle of someone "getting the ruler" with sufficient frequency to make our lives quite interesting. Otherwise we spent most of our time learning the multiplication table, which was rather hard for me (numbers have never been my thing). I had a special block about six times nine (seven times eight being a close runner-up), and was very pleased one day to come across a poem in one of my mother's old schoolbooks, that took care of my difficulty very nicely. I offer it here, in defiance of any applicable copyright law, as a public service; in my opinion it should be widely available:

> I'd studied my six times over and over,
> And backwards and forwards too,
> But I couldn't remember six times nine,
> And I didn't know what to do,
> Till Sister told me to play with my doll,
> And not to bother my head;
> "If you call her Fifty-Four for a while,
> You'll learn it by heart," she said.
>
> So I took my favorite, Mary Ann
> (Though I thought it a dreadful shame
> To give such a perfectly lovely doll
> Such a perfectly horrid name)
> And I called her my dear little Fifty-Four
> A hundred times, till I knew
> The answer to six times nine as well as
> The answer to two times two.
>
> Next day Elizabeth Wigglesworth,
> Who always acts so proud,
> Said, "Six times nine is fifty-two,"
> And I nearly laughed aloud.
> But I wished I hadn't when Teacher said,
> "Now Dorothy, tell if you can,"
> For I thought of my doll, and—sakes alive—
> I answered, "Mary Ann!"

(It occurs to me for the first time that memorizing twenty-four long lines of poetry in preference to a single two-digit number may not be the easier way for some people; but it was for me.)

For fourth grade we moved up a floor. Our teacher was Mrs. Leah Cook, whose name I thought was extremely exotic, with an Old-Testament flavor, and whom I idolized for several years for no reason that I can now recall—except that she may have seemed to me to have a somewhat steadier hold on reality, to be less a "school-teacher type," than some of my other teachers. She was, now that I think of it, the only married classroom teacher I ever had in grade school, and had a relaxed motherly way with her; most of our teachers were ladylike and a bit brittle.

Mrs. Cook taught us to do division, and read to us from *Treasure Island.* At that time, *Treasure Island* was beyond my comprehension. It was out of too different a world; not one of its referents touched familiar territory. I am sorry to say, in fact, that I never did come to terms with *Treasure Island,* though I was otherwise very fond of Stevenson. Then, later in the year, Mrs. Cook read *Heidi,* and my lifelong love affair with that book began. I could understand very well about grandfathers who lived on mountains and paid no attention to little girls (though of course at bottom they loved them dearly).

Once, while I was still in the fourth grade, I stubbed my toe quite badly playing on the sidewalk outside our house. The bulky bandage made my shoe hurt; so on the second day, without saying anything to my mother, I went barefooted to school. I remember the odd oily slightly granular feeling of the school floors against my naked soles; I felt rather wild and free, and also pleased at having solved an awkward problem all by myself. But before many minutes had passed Mrs. Cook happened to glance down, saw my shocking condition, and sent me home in a hurry to get properly dressed; school, as I said, had its standards. This was one of the more humiliating experiences of my student life.

In fifth grade we had Miss Mary Connors, a pretty and vivacious young woman whose dark sleek hairdo we girls (now preadolescent) all admired and whose somewhat affected manner of twiddling a pencil between her fingers (she always had a pencil between her fingers) we all imitated. Her class stands out for several reasons. First, that is the first and only grade in which I remember doing physical exercises every morning. I vaguely think we did do them in the other grades too, but I remember those in Miss Connors' class because they involved, at least for some months, a complicated maneuver with a broomstick: each child in turn had to come in front of the class and tie him or herself into a knot by stepping in and out of the circle made by the broomstick held with a hand at each end, twisting in between steps and bringing the stick forward or back, and finally pulling him or herself triumphantly free and flourishing the stick overhead. This procedure was timed with a stopwatch and there was a tremendous competition among all of us to be the fastest, though in my case it was hopeless from the beginning as I am almost totally inflexible and my coordination is nil. The fastest in the whole class, consistently, was a lithe wiry girl named Lorraine with no shoulders and indeed hardly any bones at all, who somehow flowed through the motions in about eight seconds flat. We girls managed to despise her but the boys must have found it hard to swallow this excellence of hers; this was way before girls were supposed to be good at using their bodies, and anything in the nature of physical prowess was thought to be strictly in the masculine domain.

Miss Connors read *The Secret Garden* to us, thus lighting another permanent fire in my bosom; and it was in her class that we were introduced to the wonders of modern medicine in the form of a little periodical booklet, with pictures like a comic book, in which certain basics of hygiene were laid out for our consideration. I remember only the discussion of diphtheria antitoxin, presented as a rebus: "ant-eye-t-ox-in," with drawings of an ant, an eye, and an ox instead of the written syllables; even at the age of nine I thought this coyness was pretty stupid and entirely confusing. And the art teacher, Mrs. Kenyon, introduced a delicious new activity called "fairy flowers" in which, following her beautiful demonstration of various imaginary and imaginative flower forms with colored chalks on the blackboard, we were all encouraged to show our own originality and all proceeded to make "flowers" as identical to hers as our individual talents permitted, and took them home proudly as our own brainchildren.

I also remember Miss Connors' class as the zenith reached by the school system in its attempt to teach us correct handwriting—at that time, the so-called Palmer method. We were each supplied with a wooden pen handle, black to begin with, into which you could fit a metal nib; the cleaning and storage of these nibs and the handling of our little ink bottles was taught in great detail and closely supervised. We were then taught how to hold the pen, with a most unnatural but elegant-looking loose grip, and warned that on no account were we to allow the hand to bend at the wrist; all motions were to be carried out by the whole hand and arm as a unit, pivoting from the shoulder. Maintaining this pose, we were drilled daily in a variety of exercises of increasing complexity, to make us expert at producing the various strokes needed for perfect Palmer penmanship: the simple push-pull, the m-loops, the u-loops, the graceful connecting loops, the o-shapes, the l-shapes; each was multiplied by our awkward little hands over several lines of specially ruled paper, while Miss Connors strolled up and down the aisles to see how we were doing and when it was time to move on to the next. When (if) a child became proficient enough at these exercises he was given the much-desired pen handle of apple-green; what a lovely color this was, how smooth it felt under one's fingers, how the light shone off its charming curves! There were, I think, one or two colors even beyond this for really superior achievement, but the green was as far as I got. With it you were allowed to go on to the Palmer capitals, miracles of beauty and proportion which, in spite of my conversion to italic in middle age, I still admire greatly as produced by an expert but never could do myself.

I think Palmer penmanship died out some decades ago, victim to the new craze for individuality. This is probably no great loss—everyone reverts to what feels comfortable in his own hand immediately on being released from school anyway—but I do have some nostalgia for those innocent days when we all sat at our desks in neat rows and made swoops and zigzags across the paper in unison, imagining our futures as little units of the State who had been properly taught. There is, for a child, a definite comfort in regimentation.

In sixth grade we had Miss Bodine; she had a younger brother who was actually a pupil in the seventh or eighth grade, and I believe this was my first clue to the fact that teachers were real people who had family relationships like other people. (We had, for several years, had a series of teachers boarding with us at home, but those ladies were definitely categorized in my mind under the genus "teacher" rather than the genus "human being"; I was too shy ever to get to know them, and in retrospect it seems likely that they too were shy as well as, probably, homesick. I perceived them only from a respectful distance, and kept this distance even in my mind, never speculating about their private lives any more than I did those of the statues whose pictures I saw in books.) About Miss Bodine, I remember only that she taught us long division, and that I had to get my sister to teach it to me all over again at home. (I still don't understand how it works, and cannot even imagine the cast of mind of that long-ago person who sat under an apple tree and created the system.)

Seventh grade, Miss Walsh: a large white-haired woman whom we had feared and obeyed, as playground monitor and halls-supervisor, since kindergarten days. I, at least, never lost an exaggerated sense of her majesty and was never really comfortable in her presence. The only thing I remember about her classroom is the enormous mural created by several of the pupils, drawn and watercolored on paper three feet wide and extending the full length of the blackboard on two sides of the room. The subject was "Cornwallis Surrendering at Yorktown," and that name and place are among the very few bits of information about the Revolutionary War that have stuck with me. I don't even remember the date of this event, as it was not included in the title of the picture.

And eighth grade, Miss Mary Carney (sister to Miss Gertrude; they had lived together and taught in the same school all their lives): another lady well along in years and with, I think it is fair to say, some deficiency of sympathy with the inner life of adolescent youth. It was with her that I first permitted myself to feel critical in relation to a teacher, and even to make a little fun of her behind her back with my girlfriends. I don't think this was due to any particular malfeasance on Miss Carney's part, it was just that I was at that age.

I was also at the age to be embarrassed by my parents, and will probably never get over the memory of the day my father was unexpectedly called in to our class as a substitute teacher. Being for some reason unprepared to go on with whatever Miss Carney had been doing in American literature, he read aloud to us the whole of *The Descent into the Maelstrom* in an outdated oratorical style that made some of my classmates giggle and the rest go to sleep. It was horrible, watching my beloved father make a fool of himself in front of the whole class. It went on and on.

Seventh and eighth grades were called junior high school and were conducted on the top floor of the building, where the rooms were for a change bright and airy. (Were there really as many floors as I recall in that little school? I certainly had a strong sense of moving *up* physically with every second or third educational level, and a sense of having arrived at the top in several ways when I got to seventh grade.) Junior high school marked the beginning of a departmental system in that, for the first time, different teachers would come in to the classroom for different subjects, so we began to grasp the idea that every teacher was not necessarily an infallible expert on every subject, as we had believed up to then. Also we ourselves were moved around, for the very grown-up functions of Gym, Home Ec, and Assembly.

Gym, for us girls, consisted of exercises in a large frigid too-well-lighted room; I hated it because of my inability in that direction though I did rather enjoy wearing the dark-green bloomers that constituted the uniform. But I took great pleasure in Home Ec (never called by its full name; I'm not sure I knew what its full name was). This was taught only to the girls; boys had Manual Training and turned up after class with little bookcases and birdhouses and picture frames; I always wished I could take Manual Training too. But Home Ec satisfied some deep feeling of wanting to learn how to be a woman, and indeed we were given good skills in some very practical domestic maneuvers.

Miss Bessie Pleasants was the teacher, a plain placid middle-aged lady whom nothing seemed to ruffle and for whom nothing seemed to go seriously wrong anyway. I have vivid memories of the things she taught us, and they have stuck with me ever since—not that all of them have proven very useful. The first lesson, and it went on for some weeks, was how to darn socks and stockings. I was quite good at this kind of fine finger-work, and my mother was delighted to have me take over (temporarily) the considerable chore of darning that occupied significant amounts of every housewife's time in those days. Not only could I fill in holes in such a way as to make them comfortably wearable and pose no strain on the remaining fabric, but I learned to mend vertical runs in stockings invisibly—or at least neatly enough to be worn for months more. Women did wear such mended stockings then; in that culture, not to continue using a garment that "still had wear in it" was looked down on as poor management. A woman took pride, not in having new or perfect stockings—though that was certainly nice too—but in the skill with which they were mended; women congratulated each other on clever unobtrusive mends and patches much as, in more affluent cultures, they compliment each other on the taste shown in selecting a becoming new garment. I was proud of my handiwork, and when I grew up and had children I faithfully mended their socks for some years, until the pressures of work outside the home caught up with me; when I cleaned out my bureau one spring and found a drawer completely stuffed with unmended socks too small for any of the children to wear, I reluctantly gave up and threw them out, knowing that no New York City mother of the 1960s, however poor and needful, would find socks with holes an acceptable or usable offering. As I closed the incinerator door, I distinctly heard the shades of my ancestors weeping.

Patching was also learned, and an enjoyable skill it is, rising to an art form in relation to matching of patterns and duplication of weave with one's needle. A nearly invisible patch is still, with me, a matter for considerable self-satisfaction, but one has to choose one's audience carefully nowadays in airing this particular accomplishment; it is no longer generally admired.

Then we progressed to making aprons—garments worn, in my youth, most of the day by most housewives I knew (meaning most *women* I knew). The selection of the prettiest floral pattern one could find (within certain well-understood limits) and the agonized choice of a contrasting binding for the edges took long, deep thought; and as the apron, though simple in design, was to stand to all the world as a loud clear statement of your womanly competence—the first such statement—it was made with a terrific amount of care. Once having achieved the necessary, useful, everyday apron, you graduated to making a pretty half-apron of gingham, which you smocked with matching embroidery floss and gave to your mother for Christmas. (All the girls made such aprons and gave them to their mothers for Christmas; the mothers did not wear them, but kept them in a drawer and showed them to other mothers, each secretly thinking her own daughter's work was superior to all the rest.)

We had cooking lessons too, in a room with row after row of little electrical stoves that seemed to me like children's toys, artificial and puny (at home we still had a wood-burning stove). Of two years of such lessons I remember only how to make blanc-mange (I came home and showed off the French word, my first, to my mother and when she found out how this stylish dessert was put together she sniffed and said, "Oh, cornstarch pudding"); plain muffins; and a dish called goldenrod eggs which I still enjoy (it is hard-boiled eggs cut up in a cream sauce, served on toast with the yolks sieved over the top to look like goldenrod).

In eighth grade we learned how to make dresses, simple cotton ones such as Deanna Durbin would wear a few years later, with little Peter Pan collars and short puffed sleeves. This was before zippers, and by far the hardest part of the dress was the placket under the arm, composed of several layers of fabric made into buttonholes on the front flap and a strip to support buttons on the back—all theoretically lying as flat and unobtrusive as if it were a simple seam. This ideal was never reached; even quite expert seamstresses turned out plackets that were more or less bunchy, just as even expensively corseted matrons showed the bony contours of their underpinnings beneath their smooth crepe skirts. It was one of those things society agreed to ignore, like sex and body odor.

Some girls, who were quick and talented, went on to make more complicated garments, two-piece suits and even shorts for summer (shorts were just coming in). I remember one Assembly at which the entertainment consisted of a "fashion show" by the eighth-graders (I was only in seventh grade at the time), wearing the things they had made during the term. Miss Pleasants was of course the commentator, easygoing and mildly twinkling as always. I remember her describing one suit as "modern—even ultramodern." She added that the older sister of the girl in question, now in high school and a Latin student, insisted that the word "ultramodern" be pronounced in the Latin way with a long "u," "ooltramodern." I was deeply struck by this extreme degree of sophistication and sensibility, and was sure I would have trouble functioning at an appropriate level when I arrived in the rarefied atmosphere of high school. I was, unquestionably, a worrying child.

Assembly took place in a large bright room on the top floor. It was furnished with the same yellow wooden desks, with wrought-iron bases of herculean toughness, that had withstood the ravages of generations of adolescents. (They were called "young people" then, thus implicitly recognizing their bond with the rest of humanity and setting forth the expectation that they would one day in the course of nature become simply "people.") There was the same dark oiled floor as in the rest of the school; at the front of the room this was elevated into a large low platform on which, week by week, a variety of entertainments were presented to us. I remember almost none of these and I think they tended to be of the morally elevating, civic-consciousness kind, lectures intended to turn us into good citizens. They might have done so had we listened; I at least did not.

What I did listen to with great interest, in Assembly, was a series of broadcasts by Walter Damrosch, then conductor of the New York Philharmonic Orchestra. He ran, for several years, a weekly (I think it was Friday mornings) "Music Appreciation" program for school children in which he expounded briefly on some aspect of music, sometimes technical and sometimes aesthetic, illustrating his remarks with specially recorded tidbits. This was my very first connection with the official world of music except for the part-singing we had been doing all through the grades. I learned about the various instruments of the orchestra and heard never-to-be-forgotten excerpts from such easily assimilated masterpieces as "Peter and the Wolf," "The Flight of the Bumblebee," "The Swan," "Anitra's Dance," and "Hungarian Dance No. 5." Mr. Damrosch began each presentation by saying, in his precise, slightly accented, and unctuous voice, "My dear children"; he thus mixed himself up, in my mind, with President Roosevelt (*the* President from the time I was nine until I was almost twenty-two) with his Fireside Chats on the radio, beginning always with "My friends." These two voices, both vaguely associated with the great and distant state of New York and both with a rich wise timbre, speaking kindly and encouragingly as if to their good loyal inferiors, constituted my mental image of those in power throughout my youth; I grew up trusting and admiring such men.

The visual arts, except for Mrs. Kenyon's weekly forays into the classroom, perceived by all of us as pure recreation (as far as I recall they included no instructional element), were neglected in the Bennington Graded School. I remember no pictures on the walls, no study of art forms from any point of view. We drew, and we painted in watercolors, imitatively, and that was all. But in Assembly we were exposed to one fine piece of sculpture, donated I suppose by some classically educated benefactor of the last century; we saw it with increasing frequency from our kindergarten days, when we used to be led upstairs and through the chuckling Assembly in our Hallowe'en costumes, to junior high when we were there for one purpose or another almost daily.

This statue stood in the well of the wide oak stairs that led, with a landing under an enormous paned window, up into the Assembly room: a life-sized marble nude representing the god Mercury. Lighted by the window behind him (he faced into the room), poised lightly on one foot, he beckoned to us—truly, in that prosaic setting, a messenger from another world. Through all the solemn exhortations of the principal and the dreary visiting speakers in their three-piece suits he was there, quietly intent on his errand; he was there for hearing tests and Special Announcements and final exams; he listened with us, gravely, to Music Appreciation (but with his inner ear tuned to a still more compelling sound). Silent, beautiful, unnoticed except for the occasional embarrassed giggle, he communicated—more subtly and more fully than our Assembly-planners dreamed of doing, so that I remember him clearly and their productions not at all—a sense of winged expansive human thought and achievement, of civilization itself.

Church

MY FAMILY WERE what is called pillars of the Congregational Church in Bennington. We attended every kind of function that was offered and participated fully in all the manifold ways that were expected; our social life was almost exclusively associated with the church and its activities. Until I was several years out of college I considered myself a "good Congregationalist." But religion had nothing to do with it, nor did anyone ever indicate to me by so much as a hair that religion did have anything to do with it.

My father had a beautiful tenor voice; he never got any professional training, but sang at home and in church—and in fact anywhere he could—all his life. In college he was a soloist with the Middlebury College Choir and thus earned part of his tuition. We were all exceedingly proud of this talent.

So of course when we came to Bennington he began singing in the Congregational Church (what else—Marshfield has been Congregational throughout its history), and was one of the four soloists who constituted the choir there for twenty-five years, never missing a Sunday that I know of. And of course his faithful wife came to church to hear and admire what she had been hearing sung around the house all week. And of course the little daughters came too, in their best dresses (such as they were) and carrying their own books to read during the long service.

My mother taught me the Lord's Prayer at an early age—I remember having vocabulary problems with it, similar to my problems with the Pledge of Allegiance. The word "trespass" was unknown to me; I heard it as a transitive verb with its object, "tresp us"; but by this reading the phrase "forgive us our tresp us as as we forgive…"

was a hopeless conundrum, and "those who tresp us *against* us" was enigmatic in the extreme. My mother never explained any of this; I never asked her. We Vermonters were shy of all such deep matters, and private in our struggles to come to terms with them.

Learning to say the Lord's Prayer was as far as my home religious instruction went (though I never doubted for a moment that my parents were faithful believers in Something); the rest was presumably to be inhaled like incense within the church itself. The trouble was, there was no incense to inhale. Our church was of plain red brick, with a plain red-brick steeple. The big room where Sunday services were held was finished and furnished in yellow oak with a high varnish. A number of tall windows with plain glass panes flooded the room with plain everyday light. In front there was a raised platform with three large carved wooden chairs in the middle and a reading desk at one side; below this platform was a big oak table with words carved around the edge in Gothic letters: THIS DO IN REMEMBRANCE OF ME. Behind the platform was a yet higher balcony arrangement where the four church singers sat, placidly facing their audience, backed by the great golden organ pipes; Mrs. Bridges the organist was hidden behind the console (you could see the pages turn sometimes if you watched carefully).

There was no cross, there were no candles and no flowers, no pictures and no statues. Not so much as an American flag. There was no procession. The minister, Mr. Cummings, wore a plain three-piece suit of threadbare black; the singers wore regular Sunday clothes. The congregation also wore Sunday clothes, musty-smelling suits and rayon dresses with faded seams and ancient handed-down finery at the neck. They came in silence and sat in silence, looking straight ahead with faces of inscrutable virtue; they were communing no doubt with Beauty bare but, good Yankees all, not giving a thing away. They did not genuflect, or cross themselves, or lean forward and cover their faces when praying, but maintained the same upright stony dignity from start to finish.

The service was of course not a Mass. We celebrated the Lord's Supper only once a month, with grape juice in thimble-sized individual glasses and cubes of plain bakery bread passed around on small round trays; after drinking your grape juice you put the empty glass in a little wooden rack fastened to the pew ahead of you. The passage from St. Luke's Gospel describing the Last Supper was read, but no indication was given that there was any more to this ritual than a simple "remembrance." I am not sure, to this day, that Congregationalists think there *is* any more to it. That church guards its independence and that of its individual members so fiercely that there is, as far as I know, no formal dogma at all; what you are there for is a totally private matter, into which no one inquires or attempts to instruct you. And if, as in my case, you are really looking for information on these points, you are just out of luck.

We sang a good number of hymns, and heard a solo or anthem by the choir while the collection was being taken. It was a "collection," not an "offering"; these were people who called a spade a spade. Then there was a dreary childish sermon (dreary even for children—Mr. Cummings was, next to my father, the nicest and best man I knew, but he was not a lively speaker), followed by a pastoral prayer and then the Lord's Prayer. At Christmas we sang Christmas carols instead of everyday hymns, at Easter we sang "Christ the Lord Is Risen Today" and Mr. Cummings preached a sermon (every year) about a butterfly coming out of a cocoon; these were the only variations in the service.

In sixteen years of attending that church I failed to grasp the central tenets of the Christian faith, since they were neither presented nor discussed. The messages I got were that it was a very serious business; that it was not to be talked about; and that everybody else knew something I didn't. (These were the same messages, incidentally, that I got about sex; and when, in later years, I began to read books from the library to fill in the gaps in my information, I learned about both subjects with a similar furtive excitement.)

Once we started school we also started Sunday School, a forty-five-minute session just before the church service. For that, we first gathered as a group around Mrs. Cummings at an old black piano in a basement room to sing some suitable baby hymn. I don't remember any of the hymns at this late date but I do remember the picture over the piano: *Suffer the Little Children to Come Unto Me*, and the one on

the wall off to the right: *All Things Bright and Beautiful.* These spoke
volumes to me, and were the best lessons I ever learned in that room.
After the song we divided into age groups, and some high school
girls and a few elderly widows steered us unemotionally through the
reading of a little four-page leaflet with quite a nice picture on its
front, illustrating the story of the week out of the Bible. At the end
of the story were printed some elementary questions designed to rub
in the moral of the story, or at least its basic facts. When there was
time left over we were given large sheets of white paper and some
well-worn crayons with the red always missing, and set to drawing
pictures of our own (we usually picked subjects totally unrelated to
the message of the day, and this seemed to be quite all right with the
teachers, who had by now administered as much moral enlighten-
ment as they felt called on for).

But—oh yes. Before we even came into this room each Sunday
there would be an assembly session in the basement auditorium, led
by Mr. Homer Webster, the president of the County National Bank
on the corner of Main Street and, by a natural extension of responsibility, also the superintendent of the Sunday School. He was a gray-
haired, gray-suited, serious-minded man with one glass eye, who
didn't move his mouth when he spoke or raise his voice in conse-
quence of speaking in a large room, and I am afraid that whatever
spiritual guidance he directed at us children was totally lost on most
of us; between our trying to figure out who he was really looking at,
and our not being able to understand a word he said, the message
was seriously compromised. Although—communication is more
than words—I will say that the image of Mr. Webster standing up
there so square Sunday after Sunday with his Bible in his hand, well-
dressed, well-groomed, glinting amiably around the room as he
spoke unemphatically and unnoticeably on, and lending the whole
situation an invincible aura of mature respectability and financial
probity, gave me and probably some others a kind of adult role
model which sank in at some level of our psyches far too deep for
conscious awareness.

Mr. Webster was, in his weekday aspect, a kindly man and a
neighbor of ours on Silver Street (he lived in one of the big new

houses at the top of the hill). He also happened to be our landlord, and once brought me home with his own hand when I had wandered off at the age of five and he caught sight of me sitting all alone on the curbstone outside his office window, half a mile from our house. So I always thought of him as, in some sense, my special hero; but neither of us presumed on this accidental association.

He was presently succeeded in the Sunday School by Mr. Walfrid Wahlquist, who was Bennington's postmaster and a very different type, though almost equally respectable. He had a long Swedish body topped by a long sad weatherbeaten Swedish face, a face intended by Nature for despairing introspection, but with a jolly boyish persona incongruously superimposed. He would bounce across the podium at the front of the room waving his Bible and holding forth enthusiastically about—what? I have not the faintest recollection. (Vermonters are in general wary of enthusiastic persons and tend not to pay much attention to their outpourings.) I liked Mr. Wahlquist; grownups who actually smiled at children were distinctly rare in Bennington, and it was reassuring. But on the whole, and from sixty years' retrospect, I think Mr. Webster's quiet dignity gave us more to feed on.

I learned a few, very few but very specific facts in those assemblies. One, a memorized statement: "The Bible is a collection of sixty-six books, telling of the search of the Jewish people after God." This took us, as a group, all one season to learn. Again in retrospect, I am struck by the humanistic tone of the statement and the lack of any indication that God was ever found. Two: The titles of the books of the Old Testament, in order—which I can still recite. (I don't know why I never learned those of the New Testament—one would think they must have been in the same curriculum—but I didn't.) These two major pieces of information plus the Bible stories we read Sunday by Sunday constitute, maybe, not too bad a harvest; I don't honestly know what one is expected to learn in Sunday School. I learned at least enough about the Bible to want to know more, and beginning in high school read it straight through for the first of several times, until I found its ambiguity so baffling that I gave up.

For six weeks every fall, just after school started, there was a weekly program in the church basement called "Schoolamissions." It is embarrassing to admit, but a true fact, that I was grown up and living away from home before it occurred to me that this enterprise was really meant to be designated a *School of Missions*, and to teach us something about what was going on in the outreaches of the Congregational Church. Schoolamissions to me meant a highly enjoyable social evening, involving family members of all ages. First we gathered in the basement and sang a hymn, "We've a Story to Tell to the Nations" or "Fling Out the Banner, Let It Float"; then we lined up in front of a half-door into the kitchen and were dealt out sandwiches and hot cocoa; we each arranged this supper on the seat of one of the wooden folding chairs and sat on another one. The novelty, glamor, and (for me) slight thrilling sense of desecration of holy places, as well as the very good and hearty sandwiches in the making of which the Congregational wives competed seriously though thriftily, made this a really festive meal. Afterwards there was a brief enjoyable scuffle as plates and cups were returned to the kitchen and the big boys with much argument and show of muscle scraped the chairs back into their tidy rows. Then we separated into age groups and there was a half-hour or so of what you might call academic work. You might, but…I think the grownups got to see slides and have discussions; we children, I vaguely recall, read little leaflets with pictures almost identical to our Sunday School leaflets, except that these purported to inform us about the quaint domestic arrangements of odd-looking people in various far-away inferior countries. But we were so full of good food and so exhilarated by the recent license granted in the auditorium, and then it was so near our bedtime, that not very much penetrated; at least not to me. I loved Schoolamissions, but in ten years of it I never got the point. (This may have been true of others too, and eventually taken official note of; the whole Schoolamissions operation was dropped during my high school years. Of course by then there was a movie house on Main Street.)

One of our Sunday School teachers, the one who took the third-graders, was Mrs. Daisy Stickles, a quiet inexpressive widow of around sixty. She must have had a warm outgoing heart in there somewhere, because she established and maintained for many years a service called simply "Club." She may have had a more hifalutin name for it; Club is what we children called it. This was a group of third- and fourth-grade girls (think of it, just ten or eleven years old), who would meet at Mrs. Stickles' house every Wednesday after school to eat sandwiches (which we brought from home in rotation), drink cocoa, and—if you can believe it—memorize Psalms, one each week, or half of a very long one. I think there was some sort of prerequisite for Club membership, probably having to do with school grades, to ensure that memorization on this scale would not be a real hardship; anyway, there were only ten or twelve of us.

Mrs. Stickles was better off than most of us girls; it was a treat to be in her (relatively) richly appointed home, sitting on her nice furniture in front of her comfortably blazing fire (another novelty), drinking out of her pretty china cups. We felt grown up and responsible, and we happily memorized all the Psalms she wanted, in return for these privileges. Thus I acquired, over two years, a substantial inner store of the most beautiful and strongest poetry in the language. It has supported me all through my life, quite independently of the fluctuations of my formal "religious belief"; I still, at times of pain and even at times of exaltation, resort to those incomparable stanzas. They speak to the soul.

Mrs. Stickles never gave one word of "interpretation," or even asked us what we thought the lines meant; she let the poetry say it all. I never spoke to her, or saw her as far as I remember, either before or after these two years. I think she did me as much good as any teacher I ever had.

The church service itself, as I have indicated, in no way advanced my spiritual understanding or contributed to any growth in virtue. I am sorry to say that the Congregational Church as I experienced it was an outright failure as a religious institution; after all those years of faithful churchmanship, what I had was an abiding sense of guilt with no vocabulary to express it, no philosophy to frame it, and no liturgy to assuage it. ("Be ye therefore perfect" was the only clear unequivocal message I got from all my Bible-reading, and it pierced me with despair.) But then, it turned out in the end that I am an Episcopalian by temperament; how was anyone to guess, in my childhood, a mortifying thing like that?

It is only fair to say, too, that the teaching and practise of religion does not seem to have been, at that period, the church's major function; not that church, at least. It provided, rather, the ground, center, and fulcrum for most of the social life of its congregation, and a group identity which clearly filled some deep need.

Take my parents. They were, admittedly, unusual in being probably the closest personal friends of the minister and his wife (who had three children of about the ages of my sister and me), so that two-family suppers, picnics, and even overnight outings were not uncommon. But it was more than that. The three people who with my father constituted the church choir also made up the nucleus of a two-table bridge club which was my parents' chief domestic recreation for nearly fifty years; I honestly don't think they would have been comfortable with any but Congregationalists in this intimate a relationship. To invite someone into your home was a letting down of the barriers of personal privacy that their generation gave way to very sparingly. (In more than forty years of living on Warn Street, my mother never set foot in any other house on the street or invited the adults from any other house into hers; they were all perfectly good neighbors, friendly and unconstrained on a back-yard, front-porch basis; but two families were Catholic, one was Baptist, and one not churchgoing. The children went in and out of each others' houses like flies and this didn't bother anybody; but the grownups "didn't visit.")

The three other choir members were the bass Howard Estes, about six feet three inches tall (my father was five feet four), who kept a high-class butchery and grocery store in the neighborhood; his wife Elsa, the soprano, a bit lively and flirtatious for the group as a whole (she was sister to Walfrid Wahlquist); and Flossie Gerken, with a most beautiful mellow contralto and a subdued Madonna-like face and personality to match, dark hair smoothly waved from a middle part and pinned into a neat bun at the nape. All these lived on Silver Street, within a few minutes' walking distance when the bridge group first started. Flossie's husband Richard, a totally silent man, made a sixth; and there was always of course one other couple to complete the two tables, but that was subject to some turnover, perhaps because the chemistry among the six "regulars" was so binding that any others felt necessarily like outsiders.

These bridge evenings seemed to me the last word in stylish entertaining. As our turn approached, my mother would pore painfully over her recipe file, trying to find something she could serve that would knock the ladies' socks off with its novelty and at the same time permit the conservative men to get it down and keep smiling; this was apt to be an idea she had clipped from a magazine, or that one of her out-of-town friends had sent her. After the group had played for a couple of hours, she would clear the tables and cover them with her best hand-embroidered cloths, serve the special dish of the evening (always a dessert, since people had already had the main part of their suppers at home) with much genteel turning of her wrist, and accept the fulsome praises of the company with repeated protestations about the inadequacy of the amount or the fact that she couldn't get any pecans and had to make do with walnuts or how she was afraid she'd left it in the oven just five minutes too long. These gambits, which might have been scorned by a more sophisticated society, were here accepted as the proper way for a hostess to receive thanks, and the lady guests' eager countering of each of her self-criticisms took up pretty much the whole time the food was on the table. The men's role was to eat heartily, to take a second helping if at all possible without damage to their insides, and to grunt at least once—with sufficient resonance to command some credibility— "Good pie" (or cake, or pudding). To accompany these rich desserts there was strong black perked coffee; this, as nobody had heard of caffeine yet, kept nobody awake at night. After that there was singing; not the church music, which they rehearsed on Thursday evenings, but selections out of the *Golden Book of Favorite Songs* or occasionally some new piece of which the Estes had brought the sheet music. But mainly it was old favorites including the songs of their own parents' youth, "Believe Me If All Those Endearing Young Charms" and "Juanita" and "A Spanish Cavalier" and "When You and I Were Young," usually with some Stephen Foster mixed in and something light and modern to finish up, "Alouette" or "Pack Up Your Troubles in Your Old Kit Bag." I used to crouch on the stairs behind the piano to listen (our piano, by the way, "came with" the house when we bought it, a wonderful piece of good fortune); I loved it when Mr. Estes, who had a gorgeously pure open bass, would do a solo of "Rocked in the Cradle of the Deep," with its final descending scale down to an incredible hollow vibrating tone that seemed almost inhuman.

Church suppers were another way in which the Congregationalists passed their time and bolstered up their collective ego. The kitchen in our church was immense, and its shelves well stocked; at the time of a supper the place swarmed with bustling housewives, each ostentatiously deferring to all the others while knowing perfectly well that her way was the only right way; the amount of practiced hypocrisy shown in the course of one of these evenings would have done credit to a Renaissance court. Potatoes boiled, and soups steamed, in the biggest aluminum pots I have ever seen; with some of them, a man had to be recruited to pour off the water when the boiling was done, though otherwise no man dared stick his nose into the kitchen until it was washing-up time. In general, women brought "made dishes" from home, having been given some idea of the category needed; these of course constituted public displays of their culinary skill, and were the subject of much soul-searching and anxious consultation.

I happen to have—it was tucked into my mother's old tin recipe box, which I grabbed after her death—her record of a church supper that she apparently masterminded, in 1942 (about ten years after the time I'm talking about, but near enough). She was, at least, the one who kept the accounts; it's all laid out, from "45 pounds corn beef, $13.05" to "9 qts. milk—$1\frac{1}{2}$ qt. cream, $1.96." There were six women in the kitchen, and two men to wash the dishes; in the dining room, there were five more women working. Sixteen women brought a total of twenty pies, and one pie was left over, which was sold for 25 cents. Tickets for this dinner were apparently about 40 cents. One hundred eighteen people were fed, and the overall profit was $22.04. It doesn't seem like a lot even for those days, for the amount of work that went into it; but you have to remember that it counted, heavily, as a social diversion for most of the women involved, and of course for their husbands and children as well. The fact that it was very hard work probably didn't even faze them; they would have been working just as hard if they had stayed at home.

As we children got up to high school age, the church ministered to our social needs in yet another way. Or rather Mr. and Mrs. Cummings did. (Mrs. Cummings was a minister's wife of the old kind, who did at least as much of the church's work as he.) They opened their house every Sunday evening, for at least the sixteen years I lived in Bennington, to high school students of any denomination who wanted to come. The result of this extraordinary hospitality was referred to as Parsonage Club. Sandwiches (brought by the youngsters in turns) and cocoa (made by a couple of the girls in the big back kitchen) were laid out on a long mahogany table with a lace tablecloth, with candles; we all stood around and sang the Doxology and then ate the sandwiches and drank the cocoa as only adolescents can. When they were all gone, three or four of us cleaned up and the others, usually numbering twenty or twenty-five, adjourned to one of the two smallish parlors, separated by a wide hallway with arches on both sides.

In this first parlor was an old-fashioned foot-pumped organ, with a hymnbook on its rack; Mrs. Cummings or any one of the girls who had had enough piano lessons would play hymns on request and the whole group would sing them with tremendous enthusiasm and volume, sometimes even with parts. We sang everything, from the hushed reverence of "Fairest Lord Jesus" to the rollicking rhythms of "Follow the Gleam," and occasionally even ventured on the Pilgrim's Chorus from *Tannhauser* at the very back of the book, which Mrs. Cummings could barely cope with.

You must not think that we were unusually pious young people; this whole evening (to my ingenuous mind at least) was for the specific purpose of getting the two sexes together and letting them look each other over without the necessity for conversation or expenditure. There was no handholding or overt flirting, but we girls certainly dressed and brushed our hair with the boys in mind and I'm reasonably sure they did the same. All of us were painfully shy and socially inadept; the school dances were agony to most of us, and our rare movie dates posed nearly insurmountable conversational challenges. But at Parsonage Club we only had to come and show ourselves, and in this simple, single endeavor we were more comfortable and more successful.

The hymn singing continued for forty-five minutes or so and then there was another change of venue: we all trooped over into the second parlor where there was a fireplace with a fire going and the Cummingses' ancient odoriferous collie, Lorna, dozing in front of it. Mr. Cummings, quiet up to this point, now got out his ukulele from college and we would sing popular songs, of which he seemed to have a full command. (The popular songs of that day were such that a minister of the Gospel *could* admit familiarity with them without blushing, and sing them without having to leave out the good parts.) He would also, on request (and there were always requests), produce a song or two from his own youth, and that is how such ragtime wonders as "Oceana Roll" and "Oh, Johnny, Oh!" got into my own repertoire, to its great enrichment.

The fire burned gradually down, the young people disposed themselves along the threadbare rug in postures ever more horizontal and looked at each other through half-closed eyes, the songs became slower and more sentimental, the dog slept or let herself be stroked as a kind of proxy, and eventually Mr. Cummings would put away his ukulele and the evening was over.

During my last couple of years in high school a few of us got up a short worship service that was held over in the church in the half-hour before Parsonage Club began. And I seem to recall that once in a while Mr. and Mrs. Cummings would hold a brief discussion with the boys and the girls separately, advising us with earnest obscurity on matters of health and morality (the chief point of these chats, I now think, was to open up the field to any youngster who wanted to stay behind afterward and bring up some personal problem). But these were temporary and, I think, irrelevant for most of the Parsonage Club attendees. It was an excellent institution, perfectly geared to the needs and abilities of its members.

My feelings about the church of my childhood are, you will have gathered, well compounded of resentment, perplexity, and warm affection. I incline, these days, to the view that it gave me quite a lot of good value after all, though by the most roundabout and unlikely paths: a sense of the universality of the human lot; of our necessary solidarity in dealing with it; of the availability of strength when it is needed; and—certainly, profoundly—of the mystery of the whole thing.

The church and the parsonage, like the school, haunt my dreams, not very often but still now and then; and when they were both torn down and a bank put up on the corner I grieved heartily.

Play

IN MY YOUNG DAYS, children found their own amusements. Adults, by and large, did not play with the young; these activities were generally seen as the province of the children themselves, taught to each child by another and thus passed down the generations. Each child also invented his own games.

By today's anxious and affluent standards we had little to work with. Toys—objects owned by the child and specifically designed and intended to be played with—were rare indeed. Most children had a ball and a pack of cards of some kind; a few had checkers and a board. Practically all boys had something that would serve as a bat, and every girl had a doll. But toy shelves were not needed. The personal possessions, aside from clothes, of any child I knew were easily accommodated in a shoebox kept under the bed, or on top of the bureau. Such possessions as we did have were cherished with ardent concentrated love, and other children's possessions, if different, were coveted with open envy. Not that we felt poor or deprived; it was just how things were—it never occurred to us that they might be otherwise. In fact, when I used to read stories about rich children, "Eight Cousins" or the "Little Colonel" series, I discounted most of the descriptions of their homes and belongings as the purest fantasy. That children should live among such scenes and own such things was—well, it was a story.

My earliest recollection of any sort of recreational activity concerns "watching the movies." This must have been before I was four, because the game took place in the house in West Charleston. My sister and I slept together in a big bed with windows on the main street of the town (a dirt road, actually). When we had been left up there to fall asleep, we would instead squirm down to the foot of the bed, lie on our stomachs, and gaze at the wall behind the bed, where the headlights of passing cars threw moving shadows. In those days, cars did not come along with any great frequency, and what with the craned-back necks and the upturned eyes and the considerable waits in between "movies," it was a fairly soporific proceeding. I remember it as going on for a long long time, but it probably didn't.

From that same time I recall watching the "big kids" playing on a swing (they wouldn't let me near it and teased me because my bloomers showed below my dress) (perfectly stylish and proper in those days, but I was still susceptible to being teased about it). I remember hanging out an upstairs window to watch what was going on in the street below, and—on one occasion—getting caught by the window sash which came down on my shoulders; I believe I wasn't found for some time. I remember watching old blind Mrs. Durgins knitting on the front porch—a memory which encouraged me, years later, to learn to knit without watching my fingers. I thought, if Mrs. Durgins could do it I could too; and so it proved. And I remember very vividly one summer day when my sister and I were playing in the street and my father came along and took us to a store where he bought us both dolls, paying with a five-dollar gold piece. I have no further memory about those dolls, though they must have been an extraordinary indulgence; I can't even imagine what the occasion could have been. Maybe he was celebrating getting his new job as an insurance agent.

The years on Silver Street comprised my middle childhood, and there I was fortunate in being part of a good-sized group of children who formed a kind of neighborhood gang. Let me see, there were altogether thirteen of us within three or four years of the same age, plus three babies who came along and served minor roles as they got big enough to be useful. None of these children (eight girls, five boys) was ever a particularly close friend of mine, but we were unquestionably a functioning group which, whenever possible, played as a group and shared a great many activities.

Most of our games were played outdoors. There were of course jump rope and hopscotch and "May I?" and roly-poly (with its fancy derivative "Alari") (these last two were rendered a bit difficult by the fact that Silver Street ran quite steeply downhill). There was Hide and Seek and its offshoots Run Sheep Run and Kick the Can (in these, when it was time to bring everyone in and start a new game, our cry was "Oley oley infree, 'fyou don't come in you're it!" I mention this because I have gathered that in most parts of the country the phrase is "Allee allee infree"; that makes more sense perhaps, but I know we said "oley" because I thought it must bear some relation to that other incantation "Holy holy holy" that we sang in church, and used to brood about it).

There was Walking on the Green Grass; this seems to have disappeared from the modern child's repertoire. It is played as follows:

You have to have at least six or seven children to make a good game, and preferably about a dozen. One child is chosen, to the accompaniment of the usual amount of squabbling, manipulating, bargaining, hideous laceration of feelings, and withdrawals from the game, to be First. On a broad lawn this child then confronts all the others across a gap of twelve or fifteen feet; they form a line and hold hands. The First Child advances toward them while singing the first line of the following verse, and retreats backward during the second line.

First Child:
> Walking on the green grass, green grass, green grass,
> Walking on the green grass on a rusty dusty day.

Group (similarly advancing during the first line and retreating during the second):
> What are you walking here for, here for, here for,
> What are you walking here for on a rusty dusty day?

First Child:
> I'm walking here to get married, married, married,
> I'm walking here to get married on a rusty dusty day.

Group:
> Who are you going to marry, etc.

First Child:
> I'm going to marry _____ (name of one of the children in the Group), etc.

Group:
>   He (or she)'s all ragged and dirty, etc.

First Child:
>   He (she)'s just as clean as you are, etc. (pointing with
>   great emphasis at some member of the Group with each
>   repetition of the word "you")

Group:
>   Well take him (her) if you want him (her), etc. (lucky
>   chosen one, beaming with self-conscious pride, is here
>   pushed vigorously across to the other side)

First and Second Child (now a small Group on their own):
>   Walking on the green grass, etc.

The sequence is repeated until there is only one child left in the original Group. This unfortunate pariah however now becomes endowed with total mastery over the next cycle, and enacts a sweet revenge by "marrying" in strict order of imagined sympathy. Knowing that this is going to happen does tend to prevent the worst extremes of taunting and pointing out the obvious that might otherwise ruin this game. As it is, it is quite a good game and can go on for a whole afternoon.

Clearly, "Walking on the Green Grass" is just "Farmer in the Dell" with a different set of rhymes and a different geometry. But we never played "Walking on the Green Grass" at school and we never played "Farmer in the Dell" at home (on the school playground, it was usually supervised by a teacher). "Walking on the Green Grass" was *our* game.

On Silver Street the houses were mostly two-story and duplex, not very large. They had roofed front porches and tiny front "lawns," mostly trodden- and played-on to the complete destruction of the grass, and roomy backyards that were all continuous with each other. Our gang, among the thirteen of us, had more or less proprietary rights over three backyards on my side of the street and five on the other side; our group games used to roam from one to the other depending on the particular topography needed. The Broughams', with a good steep four-foot grassy bank between it and the next house up the hill, was best for "King of the Hill," while the Geannelises', a broad expanse of unusually level ground, was best for playing leaf house.

If you don't know how to play leaf house—and I've never met anyone who did outside this particular group of children—it takes place in the fall, when in Bennington everybody's yard and the sidewalks and the very streets are thickly layered with fallen leaves, golden and scarlet, for several weeks. The days are getting shorter and the light is already fading when you get home from school; your legs are starting to shiver and your nose runs. The leaves on the ground have begun to decay and there is an intensely bracing smell all over town, partly from the decay and partly from the nearly constant bonfires (the normal way in that benighted age to dispose of the unwanted mountains of leaves).

At the signal "Let's make a leaf house!" everyone whose parents will cooperate goes and gets a rake from home and brings it to the chosen area. With the shrill argumentation of children at work, all available leaves are raked together into two or three enormous piles, then—in a passionate display of group process at its most primitive—several working parties are set up and each one proceeds to create a part of the leaf house, which consists simply of a floor plan outlined on the lawn by rows of leaves. There is a sitting room, often with the individual chairs and tables indicated; a dining room with its table and sideboard; a kitchen with stove, sink, and icebox; sometimes a shed as well. Because of the inherent limitations of working in only two dimensions, the house is in a modern, one-story style, with bedrooms usually at the back. There is no bathroom, nor is this lack ever mentioned; these are Vermont children, belonging culturally more to the nineteenth than the twentieth century.

The building proceeds slowly because of incompetent workmen and inferior supervisory techniques, and also because there are constant battles between the leaders of the several work-parties, whose specific territories and responsibilities were usually not adequately agreed on in the beginning. But the house does take shape, if not by supper-time then with another hour's work after supper, in the yellow light from two adjacent back porches. If it doesn't get blown away overnight, it occasionally even serves as a play house for several girls for the next two or three days, in which the usual kinds of domestic dramas are enacted until the house fairly disintegrates and some parent pays a couple of the older boys five cents each to rake it up and burn it in the corner.

Our own backyard had its special characteristics, too: up in the far corner there was an apple tree, under which children had been digging and playing for at least a generation so that it served as, and was unblushingly called, a sandpile. For some reason no other house in the neighborhood boasted such a facility, and it was here that we created those improbable miniature landscapes that children love, with steep hills and winding roads and twigs stuck in for trees; or simply dug holes as deep as we could, trying to get to China; or buried things. My sister says she and her girlfriend once buried a live kitten in the sandpile; I hope that is not true.

And our yard had another distinction, in being the passageway to the Secret Tree. This was a monstrous great oak, standing on the edge of a clearing in the woods in back of our house, five or six minutes' walk away. It must have been at least sixty or seventy years old in my day, and presumably had been found and kept a secret, in its Victorian youth, by the first boys to come across it and recognize its quality; by my time, it was well known to the entire neighborhood, parents and children alike. It was a Tree of definite character and distinction; its large long horizontal limbs, the lowest ones only a few feet off the ground, offered both challenge and shelter and were about as good a child habitat as can be imagined. We repaired there as a group, by twos and threes, and even alone (at least I did) when things got too prickly at home. The Secret Tree was in fact our clubhouse. But as far as I recall we didn't do any systematic improvement or exploitation such as would certainly occur to a child of today. We didn't bring pillows or blankets, or hang swings from the branches, or build platforms in the crotches, or have meals there; nor were there initials or hearts carved in its bark. I think it had too much of an adult persona, or maybe just too much magic, for those kinds of desecration; it was an accepting, supporting Tree but not one to be trifled with.

Curiously, I don't remember any of our group having a swing in their backyard, let alone a slide or what we called a teeter-totter. So it was a big thing for our neighborhood when my father, who always liked working with wood, built a sturdy see-saw and painted it bright red. It was named "Red Lindy" after Charles Lindbergh, who had just come back from his flight to Paris; it lived on our front porch, where from dawn to dusk it was in nearly constant use by somebody or other, either for its formal purpose, or as a climbable object, or simply to lie slanting on your stomach on and think long childhood thoughts, gazing out at Silver Street through the knobby porch railings.

We did a fair amount of swimming in the summer, although—as Bennington has no lake and the Roaring Branch does not lend itself to swimming in either its trickling or its thundering mode—it took a little arranging. The town (through the Y, probably) set up swimming lessons every summer in a quiet largish puddle called North Bennington Pond (that is what it was *called*, by everyone I knew; its *name*, officially, was Lake Paran), about five miles to the north of town. Children of all ages, from five up to thirteen or so, were bundled into an old bus and driven over, a couple of times a week for six or eight weeks, to receive group instruction from some Adonis whose name I never knew and whom I would have died rather than address.

I was, as you know by now, a shy child and, thrown at the age of five among a group of twenty boisterous and mostly unknown youngsters (my sister of course paid no attention to me at all in this setting), to undertake fearful new activities in a threatening environment, I suffered severely. All through the rest of my life, the image that recurs to my brain at times of utmost misery and friendlessness —when I am on the cross so to speak—is that of my pathetic young self floating in the shallows along with a whole line of alien others, supported on my hands with my feet feebly working the "flutter-kick," and dripping profuse salt tears into the clear fresh water. I said nothing of this trouble, and no one asked why I was crying.

I got used to it, of course; children do. And over several years I learned to swim, a good steady breast stroke that gave me confidence (though neither speed nor grace) and let me participate in the advanced delights of swimming out to the raft and jumping off its twenty-foot tower. I never was able to do the crawl with any comfort and I never could learn to dive, but I was at home in and under the water and had fun and that was the main thing. Eventually I got to know the other children, and was no longer the youngest myself; and when I had learned all the words for "Show Me the Way to Go Home" and "Let Me Call You Sweetheart" and "When It's Springtime in the Rockies," I bawled them out as enthusiastically as the rest of the mob, in the smelly slippery crackly bus seats on the way home.

Aside from these lessons, my father (who as an insurance agent was able to schedule his own time, and in any case loved making children happy) would take a carload of us for an afternoon of swimming two or three times a week, entertaining us en route with his own inimitable and highly-appreciated songs. So we got quite a lot of water play. We all wore one-piece black wool bathing suits and white rubber caps; we each had an old bath towel to sit on in the car. No other kind of clothing or equipment was available or dreamed of. On the small gravelly shore we dug with sticks or with our bare hands; in the water we lay on and wrestled with and made trains of each other's bodies rather than any inanimate objects. We didn't even use water-balls; as I have said, we were not a toy-minded culture. And of course toys cost money; and by now it was the Depression.

In winter we were lucky in our climate, which provided a welcome variety in our activities and a number of naturally occurring play materials to be exploited. Bennington is nearly at the southern border of Vermont and snow was by no means a constant all winter; still, from mid-December through March the ground was quite often covered, and big snows whose drifts remained for as much as six weeks were not uncommon. Now when I talk about winter games, you must picture us as we really looked: not little zipped-up plastic sausages, but boys and girls in their normal winter clothes. For girls this meant long underwear; long brown stockings held up (loosely) by garters; a dress or a skirt and blouse; a wool coat; and hand-knitted mittens, caps, and scarves. (The mittens were from a special, very superior pattern of my grandmother Pitkin's, which I still use for my own grandchildren.) We wore our regular shoes—nobody had more than one pair in a given season—with rubbers over them. In really cold weather my mother would sometimes put my father's knee-length woolen "golf socks" over our stockings *and* shoes for warmth; and when we went to school she would give us a hot potato from the oven to hold in each hand.

These outfits were neither waterproof nor weatherproof; we got soaked and chilled and our play periods were regularly broken up by everybody's need to get back in the house to warm up. We all suffered from chapped hands and faces in cold weather, and were wise in the ways of chilblains and frostbite. We thought this was normal; we loved the winter.

The first thing we would do after a snowfall was to make angels in the virginal expanses behind our houses. Angels are made by lying down on your back in the snow and vigorously flapping your arms and legs up and down in the same plane as the ground. The arm-flapping produces angel sleeves just like the pictures in Sunday School, and the leg-flapping creates the authentic angel skirt (I suppose it's really a chiton). A population of these heavenly creatures, all over an otherwise untouched yard, surrounded by trees heavily laden with snow on every branch and twig and by houses transformed into great beauty and purity by the blanket of white, is quite a beatific sight.

When we got tired of that, and the angels had deteriorated from the inevitable onset of snowball-throwing and puppylike tussling that the boys could not resist, we would progress to making a snowman. You couldn't always do this; the snow had to be "good packing," a bit damp and self-adherent, to make any kind of structure. When it wasn't too cold and conditions were just right, we would go to work on a snowman whose size was limited only by our ability, in cooperation, to roll his lowest ball as big as possible, and then to lift the second and third ones on top. Most of our houses were coal-heated so there were always pieces of coal for buttons and eyes and mouths; the hat was usually an old tin can or pan. Our snowmen did not have arms. I do not like snowmen with arms. Snowmen are not *sup-*

posed to have arms. And we did not name them.

When it was really good packing there would inevitably be organized a major snowfight, which might last for two or three days. Children were even recruited from other neighborhoods for these tournaments. Sides were chosen and ramparts built on opposite sides of the largest back lawn available (this was boys' work); then a long time was spent in accumulating perfectly vast supplies of snowballs, arranged in neat pyramidal piles (this was girls' work).

Hostilities were usually commenced by some impatient youth who saw an advantage in striking before the other side was quite ready; this ignited real resentment and was returned with interest, and the fight was on. Naturally the boys did most of the significant throwing; girls were not forbidden, but as their balls never reached anything in the enemy's camp, their efforts were more in the nature of generally adding to the frenzy and egging on their side like cheerleaders than in actually scoring hits. (Except for one Joanie Geannelis, who was universally admitted to be as good a thrower as a boy and allowed in all their games without cavil; she later became a nun.)

There was no strategy, no goal, and no end point to these confrontations. Sometimes one side or the other would make loud claims of having "won," but this was usually disputed and scheduled for settling by yet another conflict to be arranged the next day.

When it was very cold, and the snow was fluffy and powder-like, the normal activity was tobogganing. Here the Silver Street children were in heaven, the street running straight down at an angle of about thirty degrees from the horizontal for six blocks and then continuing on the flat for another two blocks before intersecting Main Street. When there was enough snow for tobogganing, hardly any car drivers would be foolhardy enough to attempt Silver Street for a day or two, so traffic was not a problem. Not every family had a toboggan, but my recollection is that there were plenty for everybody to have as many rides as they wanted. I particularly loved tobogganing because a timid child like me could wedge herself safely in among bigger tougher ones and enjoy a ride of tremendous exhilaration without anxiety, responsibility, or exertion.

When the toboggans and returning cars had flattened down the snow to a good hard layer, if it stayed cold enough so that it didn't melt, the sleds were brought out. Every child I knew had a sled of his own. The approved method, used by most of the boys, was to hold the sled close to your body while you got a good running start, then to slam body and sled down on the ground as a unit with one final leaping push of the back leg, and sail at terrific speed down the hill, steering with the hands on the movable bar in front. This was a bit strenuous for most of us girls. We usually sat upright, often two at a time, pushed off weakly with hands and spraddled feet (or got someone to push us), and floated down Silver Street in ecstatic gentility, the girl in front steering with her feet on the bar. These slides never palled. (Incidentally, we called the whole activity "sliding," not "sledding." "Hey Johnny, come on out and slide!")

There was another kind of sliding requiring even more skill. A smooth stretch of sidewalk would be picked and several of the bigger boys (because of their weight as well as their better coordination) would, after preliminary stamping to pack down the snow, start sliding on it (on foot) as if it were ice. At first they would get only a couple of feet along before they were tripped up by loose snow or some irregularity in the packing; but each boy's passage smoothed out a little more, and the heat of friction would melt the top snow a little bit and let it be packed down harder; and the slide got longer and longer, and harder and harder, and smoother and smoother, until—well, I have seen slides fifteen feet long, a thrill and a challenge to every child in the neighborhood and a menace to all the adult householders. When a cold spell had preserved the snow all over town for a number of weeks, few sidewalks were exempt from these artefacts; a thin new snow falling over them rendered them invisible and, one would think, potentially lethal. Yet they were never forbidden, and never to my knowledge destroyed by cautious adults.

Thinking over the wonderful times we had on Silver Street (we all learned how to rollerskate on the same steep grade), it seems remarkable (a) that these activities were allowed, and (b) that we survived them. Today's safety consciousness would certainly eliminate most of our winter fun. Yet I recall only one instance of injury among our group, a broken collarbone; and that happened to a high school student while tobogganing on the gentle slopes of the country club. We had no adult supervision in any of these sports, and we were as competitive and unthinking as children always are; but we were not physically violent children, and I think we must have absorbed some degree of general circumspection from our parents just by observation and osmosis.

To complete the catalogue of winter sports, in case you are wondering: we didn't skate (until we were older) because there was no suitable body of water nearby; and we didn't ski because skiing hadn't yet come in.

In the house our games differed from those of children today only in being less dependent on equipment and in general geared more to our status as adults-in-the-making than our status as children-in-our-own-right. We played dolls and house and store and school and doctor and library, using for props real household objects as much as we were allowed, and making do for the rest with bricks and twigs and brown paper bags or newspaper torn into appropriate-sized strips (real, new paper was a rare luxury and not used for anything as frivolous as play).

A very frequent adjunct to all these games, and often a whole afternoon's game in itself, was "dressing up" in a wonderful collection of fancy Edwardian clothes that my mother kept in two big trunks out in the shed. Because she was known to be good at sewing, she was the recipient of periodic shipments of outdated or worn clothing from various friends and relations who were either not so good at sewing or just not so badly off as to have to wear made-over clothes. My mother would sort out the things that seemed to have potential—I remember coats with fur collars for both Frances and me, cut down with great care and skill from full-sized ladies' coats, and pleated plaid skirts from a man's woolen bathrobe. What remained was quite a wild assortment: beaded crepe evening dresses with hems that dipped up and down; big-brimmed hats with feathers; a white satin purse entirely covered in pearls; a worn blue velvet house robe; a boa of something gossamery, rather raddled but still capable of being flung over one's shoulder with great dash; high-heeled satin shoes with rhinestone buckles, and dainty pale blue mules; long, broken strings of beads; one massive heavily-boned corset that provided us with endless giggles; even a few men's items, a leather aviator cap, a smoking jacket with satin lapels, a worn pair of slippers. These things cannot conceivably have been, ever, in the working wardrobe of anyone my family knew; they must have been picked up at church sales or in other "job lots," for the sake of some usable item, and sent to my mother without discrimination. They were the real treasure I contributed to my friends' recreational life; other girls had a few of their parents' old clothes, but not one of them could approach the dazzling extravagance of my two trunks. We wore them faithfully, with great enthusiasm and ingenuity of application, up to our early teens. They were a kind of peephole into a larger, richer world, a different world.

In playing dolls we were inventive too. We each had at least one "real" doll, usually with a cloth body and ceramic head; but we were not limited to these. My own best doll was a flat, cloth-covered Peter Rabbit that served as my security blanket until I was thirteen and both his ears were gone and I lovingly put him away in the back of a closet, in a shoebox, and never saw him again. He made a good baby doll because he was cuddly, and a particularly good pupil for "school" because, just as in the story, "Peter was often naughty" and required hard spanking, and it didn't hurt to spank him so that salutary discipline could be freely applied.

He was my only stuffed animal; they were not so common then as now. The other girls would sometimes contribute a Teddy Bear or a Raggedy Ann; and when we needed an even larger group we would beg our mothers for the use of a squash or two and dress them in as convincing baby-clothes as we could muster (a little strip of lace for a bonnet, a napkin pinned at the neck for a dress) and set them side by side to be a class, or a family.

Sometimes we flew even further from reality and made dolls out of wooden clothespins, the kind with a round head—on which a face and hair could be sketched in crayon—and two "legs." They were quite functional for group endeavors. And sometimes in the summer we would pick hollyhock blossoms, turn them upside down so that they resembled pastel chiffon skirts, and provide all the rest from imagination. Needless to say, the hollyhock-children led very elegant pampered lives compared to the clothespin-children, who were an upright downright hardbitten lot.

We played paper dolls quite often, although nobody I knew ever bought real paper dolls; ours were cut out from the Sears Roebuck and Montgomery Ward catalogues, of which every home had a good supply. The procedure is this: you find a face you really like, and cut it out along with the top of the torso; then you search the catalogue for a suitable wardrobe and cut that out, with two flaps at the top of each garment to hold it onto the doll's shoulders. Of course the size and stance of the clothing, as well as its style and coloring, had to be right for the head and it took quite a lot of searching. In this, as in much of our playing, the necessary preparation and creation of the play materials took most of the time available, and in fact constituted most of the fun. Sometimes we did come back and play with the same paper dolls another day, but more commonly we would cut out a whole new population.

These two mail-order catalogues, the only ones I saw or knew about for many a year beyond my childhood, filled a number of useful functions for the rural and small-town families of America. They were not only the standard toilet paper in most outhouses, but also an inexhaustible source of reading material for long evenings in the kitchen, milk and cookies at hand, feet up on the fender of the stove, whose oven would still be giving out an agreeable warmth. They kept my mother up to date (more or less) on fashion, my father on the latest in waterproof hunting boots and fly-fishing technology, and my sister and me on a whole class of *things* that were out there in the big world and that otherwise we would have had no inkling of. I pored fascinated over the ladies' and gentlemen's underwear pages, so different from the simple garments my parents wore; I pondered, at length, the marcelled hairdos of the round-faced sirens posing in their sophisticated clothes, and wondered how they were achieved, and—as adolescence approached—tried in vain to get the same look by the use of Vaseline and bobby pins on my uncompromisingly straight hair. I stared, musing, into the agreeable well-groomed faces on page after page and tried to conjure up, out of my inadequately stocked mind, a picture of the lives these people must lead, the way they must speak and move, the exotic activities they must go in for in their snappy just-pressed suits and their saucy little feathered hats designed to show one whole side of the perfect waved head. They say we who grew up in that underprivileged age had no TV; ah, but we had Sears Roebuck and Montgomery Ward, and they served quite as well as soap operas and space cartoons to focus our childish dreams and give us a sense of "somewhere," "someday," "somehow."

We played cards, if anyone had a pack of Flinch or Old Maid; and then we played *with* cards. Flinch was the best game to own because it had an enormous pack, at least three times as many cards as Old Maid, and we could make vast card houses, two and even three stories high, with the most grandiose extensions and passageways. Sometimes we would use the Flinch cards just to lay out a ground plan, like a leaf house, and would then borrow face cards from my parents' bridge pack, to be people, and play "house"—or more properly "palace"—with them. (They were so obviously people of an exalted station in life that their stories tended to the heroic in scope and to the sketchy in detail, and were apt to founder for lack of information as to what a real Queen would be likely to do next in a given situation.) I liked being the Jack of Hearts best: that perfect profile! that adorable mustache! that exquisite absorption in the unseen middle distance! I thought he was a true aristocrat and a highly romantic figure, and delighted in playing his part, with the courtliest language I could summon up.

The boys in our group were very good with slingshots and spent a lot of time working at this skill (they used only inanimate targets, I am glad to say). And the older ones used to make a much-admired variant on a slingshot; it was called a rubber-band gun and was created from a block of wood about three by six inches and maybe three-quarters of an inch thick. Strapped tightly to one end with multiple strong rubber bands (narrow sections cut from an old inner tube) was a long clothespin split down the middle, its pointed top just abreast of the edge of the block itself and its rounded end projecting below to form a sort of pistol handle; a long sturdy nail formed a "trigger." You took one more inner tube section and stretched it over the distal end of the wooden block, then squeezed its two sides together and caught this loop between the clothespin and the block-end. The loop was thus held under a good deal of tension, until you "pulled the trigger"—which moved the butt-end of the clothespin forward and its pointed end backward—which released the rubber band—which flew toward its target with an amount of force that depended on how tightly it had been stretched. Only the big boys had strong enough hands to enable the use of long enough blocks to get really good action this way, but smaller boys, and even girls, kept trying. This was as close to toy guns as any of us got, except for cap pistols on the Fourth of July—for that occasion one or two of the boys would usually have a pistol and the rest would borrow it, or would just explode their caps by hammering them with stones on the sidewalk.

Marbles were very popular with both boys and girls, and great fortunes in them were made and lost weekly; Edna Brougham, a lean dexterous girl, was said at one point to have eight Quaker Oatmeal boxes full of them. To have so many that you needed even one Quaker Oatmeal box was the mark of having arrived as a marble-player to be reckoned with; most of us duds got along with only five to ten at a time, rarely risking them except to play with other duds where there was at least a fair chance of winning. We made up in intensity of appreciation what we lacked in quantity though: we gave names to our few marbles, and fingered them, and gazed into their ineffable depths, and indulged in hotly supported contentions of relative beauty and worth.

Among the boys a new marble game rose one year to fever peak. A boy would get a wooden cigar box (that very useful, adaptable, and universally available container) and with his jackknife (all boys had jackknives in those days and I don't think it occurred to anyone that they had the potential of being used as weapons)—with his jackknife, I say, he would create a neat hole in the lid, never more than an inch in diameter and sometimes barely wide enough to admit a standard small-size marble without friction. He put a few marbles in the box and then approached other boys with a challenge: to stand erect with one foot on each side of the box and drop a marble from chest height straight down, through the hole and into the box. When a marble went in, the successful boy retrieved it and took another one too, as his prize; if it failed to go in, the owner of the box picked it up and kept it as *his* prize.

There were boys who practiced this skill for hours every day for weeks; they became nearly infallible at getting the marble into the hole, and accumulated great riches. Presently, the hierarchy of skill was so well established and universally known that only a virtuosic few stood any chance of winning, and the others were afraid to try; so the bottom fell out of the market and the game died away.

In a different summer the rage was for "making powder." Two or three children would scour the neighborhood yards and streets for stones of different colors; then several enjoyable hours were spent sitting on the sidewalk smashing each stone, with a hammer, into small pieces, and then grinding the pieces between two harder stones until the residue was as fine as possible. The "powders" thus created were scraped into individual envelopes cunningly made of stiff paper in such a way that the powder would not sift out—people knew how to do such things before Scotch tape came along—and each maker's product was closely scrutinized for brilliance and originality of color and delicacy of texture. And then the trading began: first among each other, then among other children who were sought out for the purpose. Some would trade eagerly, a couple of paper clips perhaps or a small ball of "tinfoil" for a smidgen of pink dust; others would be inspired to make their own powder. This play kept a lot of us outdoors and out of trouble for some weeks, until the novelty wore off and the geological resources of the area had been exhausted.

Another "street game" was in fact a kind of community celebration, among the children at least. Every spring the tarred surface of Silver Street had to be restored after the depredations of the winter weather, and some days in advance of this event sizable piles of sand would be deposited on the sidewalk at intervals, on both sides of the street. For us children, most of whom never saw the seashore and none of whom had a real sandpile, this was an invitation to glorious dissipation. Old bent spoons and maple-sugar cans were frantically begged from our mothers; a few precious toy soldiers and cars were pulled out from under beds and supplemented by clothespin-people; cigar boxes were strategically arranged and propped to serve as barracks, garages, schools, and stores. Each sandpile then became, for a few heady days, a thriving and various community complete with wars and rumors of wars—only to be shoveled down in its pride and scattered onto the road by a still higher civilization.

When we lived on Silver Street, people did not yet have refrigerators. In winter, perishable foods were kept in some appropriately cool part of the house, usually the shed out in back. But in summer the insulated kitchen icebox was a necessity; it was kept cold by a big block of ice, delivered twice a week by an old Negro man, Mr. Ed Adams, and his son, out of a horse-drawn cart. (These were the only two black people I ever laid eyes on before I moved away from Bennington at the age of twenty; nor was I acquainted with any literature or other representations of Negro life and being, except for a generic sketch or two in a dictionary or schoolbook. I was too intimidated by these unusual fellow humans to look at them directly, and of course we did not speak to them or they to us, so I never learned anything from my own observation either.)

When the ice wagon's bell was heard down the street, we all ran into our houses for pieces of brown paper torn from grocery bags, and then out to the wagon where we stood as expectant as sparrows. Mr. Adams, using his heavy pick, would split off from the enormous blocks of ice on his wagon a hunk of suitable size for the house he was supplying next, and we would each rush to pick up one of the big splinters that shot off, wrap one end securely in brown paper, and trot away with a comfortable and delicious "sucker" that lasted for quite a while. There always seemed to be enough splinters of ice for everybody; Mr. Adams must have had a kind heart. (He was in fact a recognized hero in the town, having saved thirteen people from drowning in the spring of 1927 when the Branch flooded with more than usual ferocity; but I didn't know that then.)

We ate icicles the same way in the wintertime, but the appeal of ice in January is less than in July.

I am reminded, by all this talk of eating and of sandpiles, of the saying commonly quoted and (by me, at least) seriously believed in my childhood: "You got to eat a peck of dirt before you die." I suppose, now, that this phrase was first used to comfort someone who felt degraded or contaminated by having accidentally gotten a bit of dirt into his mouth. But I was a singularly gullible child, tending to believe just what I was told; the idea that people sometimes said what was not so penetrated to me only much later on. The meaning of the phrase was quite clear, you *had* to eat a peck of dirt before you died, so I never asked anyone for explanation or elucidation; I quietly, bravely, hopelessly worked away at my peck at odd moments, taking pinches of soil as small as possible and running into the house for a glass of water to wash them down, so as to get it over with and have the rest of my life free. I retained this superstition until I was at least eight years old.

The things children will believe! That line about "step on a crack, break your mother's back"—is it still current? And do susceptible children still find themselves immobilized in a house with bare plank floors, not being able to go anywhere at all without stepping on cracks? This is a very strong taboo, probably because most children have an indwelling sense of guilt about their mothers anyway; but it wears itself out through sheer impracticability.

Another notion, that I think I invented for myself in the depths of my obsessive little brain, required me to supply all the missing sounds that people left out in their ordinary casual speech. Someone would say "Wasn't that great?"; I would mutter under my breath "o." Someone would say "I'll go"; I would mutter "wi." I put in all the missing g's and all the full names of people normally addressed by a nickname; I remember getting quite frantic on the stairs at school, waiting in line to be admitted to the classroom, trying to keep up with three or four conversations at once and still keep it inconspicuous (because of course this was an intensely private thing, between me and my inner imperative). This one too lasted only briefly, though it did recur from time to time for a couple of years.

Bennington was not without the accouterments of civilization; it was actually a bustling town, by far the largest in its corner of the state, and the center to which neighboring towns looked for sophistication and leadership. There was an excellent public library with a large and well-stocked children's section, where a number of us stopped in as a matter of course on the way home from school each day. It provided our main reading matter aside from catalogues and the voluminous "funnies" that came with the Sunday papers some families indulged in. These "funnies" (comic books were not yet invented) were saved and shared and read over and over. My memories of *Tillie the Toiler* and *Winnie Winkle* (both of them early and beloved role models), *Moon Mullins, The Timid Soul, Bringing Up Father, Mutt and Jeff, Popeye* (that one was painful to me because it led inevitably to tiresome jokes about my name, but I loved *Popeye* just the same), the *Toonerville Trolley, Gasoline Alley, The Katzenjammer Kids, Barney Google,* and *Blondie* are nearly as vivid as those of the flesh-and-blood people I lived among at the time; they were full of realistic human frailty and entirely lovable.

And we did have a Main Street full of stores to be wandered in and out of, though of course we weren't welcome in some of them unless we actually came to buy, which was rarely the case. Mostly we would "go downstreet" as a recreation in itself. A Woolworth's, a Fishman's, and a Grant's gave us endless opportunities for comparison shopping; all were still literally five and ten cent stores where we bought most of our presents for our families, and located items that we would find acceptable when it was our turn.

Main Street, and South Street which was its major intersection, boasted several clothing stores, of less interest to us—except for Drysdale's. That up-and-coming emporium had a fascinating system of electrically operated chutes to send the customers' bills whizzing through the air up to the office in the corner of the balcony and bring the change whizzing back down, throwing sparks and setting off little bells en route, as good a show as anyone could want on a dull summer afternoon. Then there was Quinlan's drugstore, with a high glass shelf packed with old-fashioned apothecary jars on whose ornate hand-painted labels were written in Gothic letters things like "Pulv. lic." and "Aqua fortis"; also a soda fountain where on rare occasions we would spend five cents for a double-decker cone dipped in chocolate shot. There was Mr. Geannelis's candy store where we could watch him (through the window) pulling hot masses of colored sugar taffy out into long loops, sometimes pink with peanut butter inside (these were called peach blossoms), sometimes with multicolored strips for Christmas (he could make both the plain lozenge shapes and the luxurious ribbon candy out of this, all by hand); or dipping his cashew clusters into hot chocolate; or smoothing out the vast spreads of peanut brittle on his marble counter. Mr. Geannelis's candy was far too expensive for children ever to buy (though the first money I ever earned, ten cents for an hour of housework, at the age of thirteen, went for one of his cashew clusters); from his store we would go further along the street to Satter's, a small dark grocery with a long glass case on the left-hand side devoted entirely to penny candy. I don't remember Mr. Satter's face very clearly, but there is a short, dark, bearded, white-aproned Somebody there in my memory, showing unbelievable patience as we children scrutinized his entire stock (which we already knew by heart), from bulk milk chocolate to hard candy in every conceivable variation, to licorice sticks to all-day suckers both hard and chewy, to perfectly enormous spongy pillows of bubble gum with riddles on the wrappers; finally giving up our one or two sweaty pennies for a nice paper bag containing the chosen treasure, and squabbling all the way home about who would get how much of it: "You promised!" "I gave you some last time!" "I like cherry ones *more* than Helen does!" "All right for you then, all right for you!" I can hear us now.

When I was seven or eight, a new thing began. On Saturday afternoons in the summer, large numbers of children would troop down to an old barn on Union Street (there were still quite a few of these barns and stables out behind people's houses—we weren't so very far into the automotive age) and pay five cents to sit on splintery bleachers and watch Charlie Chaplin movies. This was a brand-new mode of experience for all of us, and (speaking for myself) there was a good deal of stress in adapting to it. The people on the screen did not look like any people I had ever seen before; they moved too fast, and too jerkily, so that I had trouble following the action. Then the situations and events were so beyond my experience that I was disoriented and intimidated. And between the sorrows and sufferings of the beautiful young ladies, and the equally heart-rending frustrations and yearnings of the peculiar little foreign man—not to mention the really terrifying lust and greed and cruelty of the villains—the whole business affected me like a glimpse into a previously unknown Hell.

We saw various early cartoons too; I remember the first one, showing a monstrous lion chasing a particularly small timid mouse. And we saw Lillian Gish and Mabel Normand and Buster Keaton and all the rest. How they did suffer, even the so-called comedians, falling and being kicked and eternally persecuted in one way or another. The famous scene where Harold Lloyd clings to the hands of the clock high above the city street was pure agony. I had only the dimmest understanding of the "make-believe" character of these events; I was appalled and terrified that such things could be, and that people could laugh at them.

Had it been up to me, the movie industry would have died there and then. I liked *Our Gang,* but all the rest scared me; I had nightmares. It was just too strange a world. And then there was something about the whole barbaric environment of our viewing, the rough uncomfortable boards we sat on, the constant danger of falling through, the boys who pulled your hair ribbons off in the gloom, the spiders....

But of course I kept on going, and learned what was considered funny, and got used to it. And after a couple of years a proper theater was established on Main Street, where you could sit in the ten-cent luxury of plush folding seats with arms; this was the General Stark Theater (named for the same man Starksboro was named for). Here I watched as the movies gradually got smoother and less naked in their display of human passion, more intellectual and less horrifyingly physical in their comedy, and acquired first sound and then color, and lost nearly all relation to the real world; and I became, in the end, an abysmal addict.

Movies were not the only public entertainments offered. Saturday-night-on-Main-Street was a popular diversion with both families and young couples; it involved strolling up and down in second-best clothing (the best was only for church), eating popcorn from the shiny red popcorn wagon in front of the bank (there was a little metal manikin leaning over the popper-cover, who bent forward and back as the machine turned, as if he were providing the motive force for the whole operation) and saying hello (rarely more) to the people you knew, in carefully graded degrees of cordiality depending on whether they went to your church, or were your neighbors, or whether you knew them from their place of work, or whether they were just familiar faces (the latter got a nod and what passed for a smile in Bennington, but no spoken greeting).

And we had parades at the drop of a hat, with the high school band and the girls who had learned how to twirl batons, and the Elks and the Masons and the Volunteer Fire Department and the Boy Scouts and the eighth-graders who had made a poster. The Hallowe'en parade included every child in town who could walk five blocks, dressed in the most brilliant costumes they could devise (parents didn't get involved with this). My sister and I usually draped ourselves in something slinky from our dress-up trunks and pretended to be the Queen of Sheba or a witch. We had a parade on Memorial Day and the Fourth of July and Bennington Battle Day and Armistice Day, all featuring veterans in their uniforms and speeches on the Post Office steps or out on the Alumni Field. School children would recite poetry and everybody would pledge allegiance to the flag, and we would sing "America the Beautiful" and we were all, I truly think, exalted with patriotic pride and fervor. And as these occasions were not spoiled by protest demonstrations or complicated by public discussions of the moral derelictions of our leading citizens, our satisfaction was unmixed and our feeling for our country strong and pure. (I speak for the children; I am not quite sure about the adults.)

Circuses came to Bennington almost every year, staying usually just one day, with two performances. We had no good lot for a big circus so there were only one or two rings, but when I took my granddaughter to the Ringling Brothers, Barnum and Bailey show at Madison Square Garden last year, I saw nothing generically different from what I had gasped over in Morgan's Lot sixty years before. A circus is a circus, and for an unsophisticated audience the details are really not important. Carnivals came, too, with rides and sideshows and smells and cotton candy and people whose weary filthy preoccupied patter and posturings were depressing even to me, the quintessential bumpkin, eager to believe they were angels and happy in their Paradise.

Once in a while our church would put on a special kind of church supper, consisting of an afternoon's outing at Lake Shaftsbury. Shaftsbury was some nine or ten miles north of Bennington and the lake was bigger and clearer, with a much better beach, than North Bennington Pond. Families pooled for the ride up. There were usually one or two fair-like competitions such as a greased pig or a pie-eating contest; but the main activities of the day were just swimming and eating.

Changing in and out of bathing suits was done in the cars, to save the fee of the rooms provided by the management; all cars at that time came with heavy plush curtains on their windows that could be pulled together for complete privacy. (It was stifling in a car thus closed up, and very hard to peel off wet wool and come out looking well-groomed in your picnic clothes, but we did it.) ("Picnic clothes" meant fresh, starched, and ironed cottons for women and children, and often ribbons in the hair for girls; the men commonly wore knickers with fancy socks, or simply old—but mended, clean, and pressed—pants and shirts. And, of course, hats: straw if they had them, more often their regular felts.)

Something for the meal was brought by each family, on the pot-luck system, and very rich and filling this food was; by the time you had sampled five or six of the main dishes and the corn on the cob and a couple of pies, you knew you had been fed. Salads were not fashionable yet—a woman who brought a salad to this kind of picnic would have been considered "mean" in the extreme. There was of course no alcohol. There was never any alcohol anywhere, in the society I grew up in. I don't think this had much to do with Prohibition; I think it went way back to the Puritans.

Anyway, we all ate about four times as much as was medically advisable, and then we children dabbled our feet in the water a little more and played hide and seek among the pines in the twilight while the men pitched horseshoes or played softball and the women packed up the food; and when it began to get really dark people crammed back into their cars and drove home. This was a very good kind of occasion.

Food

LIKE COUNTLESS CHILDREN before and since, I disliked much of the food I was given to eat. And indeed I was a skinny child; the "health reports" from school (in the shape of a milk bottle) that were tucked into the envelope holding our monthly report cards regularly bewailed my underweight condition, and I was among the many whose parents were specially urged to take advantage of the offering of a pint of milk in midmorning, in the classroom. This milk was delicious, as was all the milk then, with plenty of cream on top; homogenization, with its potential for disguising the removal of a considerable amount of cream, was not yet practiced. You could push your straw through the layer of cream and suck up all the skim milk from underneath, and then revel—for as long as the teacher would let you stretch it out—in a couple of inches of pure butterfat, whose delectable flavor coated your tongue for some time afterward.

We all drank plenty of milk, and yet we were all skinny kids as I remember us. I don't think this was due to inadequate *amounts* of food so much as its being, on the whole, just not tempting enough for us to eat more than was good for us. And then we were physically very active; even a bookworm like me walked a couple of miles a day to school and back, and regularly played active running and jumping games during practically all the daylight hours. We would have had to stuff ourselves outrageously to get fat.

The mainstay of the diet my mother provided, which was patterned originally on that of rural northern Vermont, was potatoes. We had potatoes at least twice a day, most commonly boiled, sometimes fried (in lard), on special occasions mashed or scalloped, rarely baked. We ate no rice except for rice pudding, and no pasta except for elbow macaroni cooked with cheese; exotic grains from other lands were unheard of. The bread in our house was almost invariably homemade; my mother made particularly good bread (always white), using water that potatoes had been boiled in. Other families were beginning to use "boughten" bread, but we liked my mother's best. When toast was wanted, it was made by removing one of the metal griddles from the top of the (woodburning) stove and holding the bread, in a wire frame with a handle, directly over the glowing lengths of wood. This procedure took close attention and quite a long time, but it made wonderful toast, with a distinctive charcoal-grilled kind of flavor.

My mother also made, fairly commonly, graham (whole wheat) muffins in cast-iron "gem pans"; the same pans were used for corn muffins and popovers, all of which came out in a charmingly rounded rectangular shape that was easy to hold and to get into your mouth without losing any butter or any crumbs. I don't know why that shape went out of fashion; it was both attractive and functional. Johnnycake (not a real corn bread, just a gruel of corn meal, salt, and water cooked in a frying pan in a thin layer, resulting in a large crisp round wafer) was a favorite of mine too, taking well to slathers of butter. And then there were baking-powder biscuits, which have all but disappeared from today's cuisine; my mother's were unspec-tacular and even a bit indigestible, but some women could make baking-powder biscuits that were ambrosial, gently browned on the outside but breaking sensuously open to reveal a pure white manna that really did melt in your mouth. These were the basis for a variety of fruit shortcakes, but were often served as a hot bread with supper too.

Upon this firm carbohydrate foundation were erected the three daily meals: breakfast at seven-thirty (everybody up and dressed), dinner at twelve, supper at six, all of course eaten at home by all members of the family together. Breakfast was hot cereal, usually oatmeal that had cooked all night on the back of the stove; as I ap-proached adolescence and became a rabid admirer of Tom Mix, who endorsed Ralston, I switched—not because I liked Ralston especially, but because you could save up the boxtops and send them in for toy

guns and makeup kits and bandanas—everything you needed to become a real cowboy.

Meat was a sometime thing. My mother used to tell about how,
one evening during our first week in Bennington, I (aged not quite
four) was sent to call my sister in for a meal and was heard by all the
neighbors: "Frances! Come on in, there's *meat* for supper!" My
mother always followed up this story by saying, with a self-conscious
titter, that—of course—meat was really not all that rare on our table;
my own memory is that it was not all that frequent either. In winter,
salt pork fried and served in crisp slices with boiled potatoes
drowned in "milk gravy" (a thin white sauce) was a standby; so was
corned beef, usually served as the center of a "boiled dinner" (a variety of root vegetables, all boiled together with the meat, the entire
meal spiced up with homemade horseradish that would bring tears to
the eyes of even my grandfather Hulett), or its invariable aftermath,
corned beef hash (whose name we did *not* change to "red flannel
hash" when it included beets). Dried salt beef, in a thick white sauce
on toast, was an occasional treat.

The chicken industry had not yet arisen in its modern
depersonalized form; chickens were legitimate "critters" and bought,
prepared, and eaten with a certain deliberate sense of ceremony. They
were relatively expensive and we had them only on occasional Sun-
days or when there were visitors. They were cooked in two ways
only: stuffed and roasted, or as chicken pie. These chickens had lived
full, free, and varied lives and had used their muscles the way God
intended; most of them I think were layers past their prime. They
had a flavor as different from that of Mr. Purdue's sanitized product
as the flavor of venison is different from that of beef. The stuffing
that went into their capacious interiors came out really tasting of
chicken; the gravy made from their drippings, and from the ground-
up giblets, needed no boosting with a bouillon cube to give it
strength (not that bouillon cubes were available or dreamed of yet).
They were cooked a long time, to subdue their magnificent flesh,
and they came to the table royally transformed, truly food for a king,
at least it seemed so to me. The chicken pies were made with a perfectly tremendous amount of gravy, and topped with baking-powder

biscuits for the final cooking; the tender chicken, the savory gravy, and the succulent soft undersides of the biscuits, all melting into the accompanying mashed potatoes and small boiled onions, combined into a meal that was rightly and reverently thought of as a feast.

In summer the chief meat I recall was ground beef, which my mother made into patties or cooked loose and served with a thin gravy on top of toast, or in the form of a dish quite popular at this time, which I distinctly recall as "Grandma Pitkin Dish" but which appears in my mother's recipe box as "Mackintosh Dinner" (Mrs. Mackintosh was a Silver Street neighbor whose long-haired husband Douglas spent most of his time looking out of a back upstairs window and talking to God; his intense, bearded countenance gave me my earliest mental image of the Hebrew prophets). This meal is an agreeable mélange of hamburger (fried loose), onion, potatoes, and tomatoes, with enough water added during the cooking to keep it all from burning and to maintain a ragout-like consistency. Mrs. Mackintosh's version further stretches the meat by adding a can of red kidney beans, but my mother—still under the influence of Grandma Pitkin, maybe—never did this.

Grinding of foodstuffs, by the way, was done in a wonderful contraption called a meat-grinder. You put a half-cup or so of the material to be ground into a funnel-like port on top, and then turned a handle which rotated a heavy screw that forced the stuff through a grating with openings of the desired size. I used to gaze down through the port at the moving screw and try vainly to imagine where the flange *came* from in the back and where it *went* to in the front; it seemed to me a mechanical impossibility. I can't say I ever really worked it out. It has, for me, the same disorienting effect as the Möbius strip they tell you about in physics class, with only one side—but you can *see* two sides with your own eyes! Well, that's another subject.

Of pork we had, besides the salt pork, occasional bacon and, even more rarely, sliced sausage (this was usually a gift from some farmer friend). My parents were also fond of liver and tripe, both cheap at that time; these are not of course foods that children can be expected to enjoy, and Frances and I would manage on bread and butter those days. Deli meats—the very word "deli"—did not exist. You will have noticed no mention of hams, roasts, steaks, or chops of any kind; I do not remember eating these at home as a child. Quite a lot of lard was taken in one way and another, and a surprising amount of butter, so our cholesterol intake must have been fairly high in spite of the skimpy meat ration, but it doesn't seem to have stuck to our arteries to any great extent; both Pitkins and Huletts were and continue to be a long-lived lot.

We had little fish, being far inland. Salt cod, soaked and served in the everlasting milk gravy with boiled potatoes, was fairly frequent; so was mackerel (at five cents a pound), which my mother split and stuffed as carefully as a chicken. But the fish that stands out in my memory, and that I think we did have with some frequency during the spring and early summer, was brook trout, brought home by my father in time for breakfast after getting up at four-thirty in the morning for the fishing expedition that was his favorite recreation. Those trout, only an hour or two out of the stream, dipped in corn meal, fried in butter and served on toast, are among my most vivid culinary memories sixty years later. Once in a while, in the sanguine glow of good red wine in a fine restaurant, I still order "brook trout"—hoping against hope to be at least reminded of the honeydew I fed on in Paradise—but it is not the same.

Eggs helped to fill our protein budget (as they call it nowadays); we didn't have them for breakfast, but often fried or scrambled for supper, or hard-boiled in a white sauce, over toast. When there were no eggs we had just the toast with white sauce, or even with plain milk (this latter was called "milk toast"); and on a few really desperate occasions I have eaten a dish called "wet toast" which is toast dipped quickly in a pan of simmering salt water and eaten with butter and salt. Montpelier crackers too, those almost unchewable, hard, dry, tasteless old-fashioned crackers about the size and heft of English muffins, which we all nevertheless adored as they were good with butter—great with cheese—and tremendous with peanut butter and jelly, were quite commonly dipped in hot green tea and then eaten with a fork, again with butter and salt; really not a bad supper dish.

Cheese was always available, good strong Vermont cheddar (in fact so strong that, as a child, I wouldn't eat it); the grownups ate it by carving a thin slice directly from the wedge with a paring knife, and carrying it to their mouths on the knife blade. (My grandfather Hulett ate much of his food from a knife blade, using the fork only to make as high and firm a pile as possible.) Macaroni and cheese was a frequent supper dish, made with the same cheddar. And we had "Dutch cheese," now called cottage cheese. No imagination at all was used in presenting it; it simply appeared on the table, ungarnished, in a sauce dish, surrounded by a little pool of its own whey; it was often a bit smelly and sour-tasting, not having been treated with artificial preservatives. I found it unpalatable.

Then of course there were baked beans. My mother's were considered especially delectable, so much so in fact that for one period of several years she "took orders" for beans and was supplying them to ten or twelve other households every Saturday night. They were boiled first, and then baked all Friday night and all day Saturday in my mother's biggest dishpan, in a slow oven with molasses and salt pork. I didn't happen to like them very much, though I can vividly remember their wonderful perfume and the way they would keep forming a thin, crackling, mouth-watering crust on top, which my mother would repeatedly stir in. At the same time, for hours on Saturday, the brown bread (a heavy concoction of whole wheat flour, suet, molasses, and raisins, packed into tin cans and cooked by steaming) would be simmering away on the top of the stove; the kitchen, which was a small one, was like a sauna: delightful in winter, miserable in summer. (I did like the brown bread, which was quite sweet and extremely filling, especially with the thick layer of butter I put on each slice.)

In the summer we had plenty of fresh vegetables: my mother grew, in a small garden in our backyard, tomatoes, peas, green beans, corn, carrots, beets, lettuce (looseleaf only, eaten with plain vinegar as a dressing), cucumbers, cabbage, and radishes. Zucchini was not yet known, nor did we use summer squash; potatoes and onions were available and cheap all year in the grocery store. All these vegetables, except the lettuce and radishes—and the peas, which we ate up as fast as they matured—she canned for winter use, and these were almost our only winter vegetables. Even the cabbage was laboriously sliced by hand and salted away in a big barrel to turn into sauerkraut (though, come to think of it, that happened only after an Austrian music teacher came to town in a WPA program and expanded our horizons in a number of directions). I think my mother got enormous satisfaction and pride from the shelves of neatly labelled Mason jars down in the cellar, as winter approached; she should have, it was absolutely dreadful work, done on a small woodburning stove in the heat of August, much of it. I remember her red face (my mother, like many redheads, was normally pale and freckled but flushed easily with exertion or excitement) and the grimaces with which she would fish out, with a spoon and her bare hands, one steaming jar after another from the boiling kettle—so like the grimaces of my grandfather milking the cows. I never thought of these two as resembling each other except in the throes of such domestic efforts.

It is a curious fact that soups played only a minor part in this cuisine; you would think that frugal country people would have lived on soup, but it was not so. My mother made no meat-based soups at all. But in the summer she made soups consisting of vegetables boiled in milk: potatoes and green beans, potatoes and peas, potatoes and corn, always with a little onion. She also grated cabbage and boiled that in milk. These are all tasty and delicious soups, and very easy to make, which I have never seen described in any cookbook; I recommend them. Corn bread goes particularly well with any of them.

After a whole winter without fresh vegetables, my mother's taste buds would perk up in the spring as soon as dandelions were seen. We would take the car and go off into some field on the edge of town, and she and my father would dig up a whole bucket full of dandelion plants with sharp little knives while my sister and I made "suckers" out of the flower stems. (To do this, you split the stem in four places, three or four inches back from the cut end, then rotate it rapidly back and forth in your mouth, whereupon the strips of stem, exuding a frightful astringency that puckers your lips, curl up into the distant semblance of an all-day sucker which you continue to lick complacently as the taste gradually becomes bearable and finally disappears.) The dandelion leaves were boiled and eaten with vinegar, but not by me.

We owed our fruit intake also to my mother's efforts. A major fruit was rhubarb, of which she had four large clumps at the back of the garden. I can hardly believe it now, but my sister and I and our friends used to cut stalks of rhubarb (with permission of course) and eat them raw as a pleasant afternoon snack. Most of the rhubarb, though, got canned and served either as "sass" (a side dish with the meat course) or in pies. In the summer we would make family trips in the car out to Trainor Meadows on the slopes of Bald Mountain, and would spend all day picking wild blueberries; later, there would be similar expeditions to the Everett Orchards south of the town where, if you picked your own cherries off the trees in August and apples in September, you got them at a substantial discount. We girls loved these outings, though we got tired of picking after a while.

We seldom saw citrus fruits. There was always an orange in the toe of each Christmas stocking, but we didn't have them at any other time (or juice either); grapefruit was quite a rarity; lemons were used only for lemonade in summertime. If a recipe called for lemon juice, vinegar was automatically substituted (the recipes my mother brought with her from Shaker Hill never do call for lemon juice, always vinegar). Once in several years, my mother would, as a very special thing, save up some grapefruit and lemon rinds and boil them in sugar water; cut into fine strips and dried so that they became hard, granular, and suckable; these were a much-loved kind of candy for us children. I don't recall our ever having grapes until my father planted some Concords out by the garage, after which (several years after) we became grape purveyors to families for blocks around. Raisins were used a great deal, in cooking and as snacks.

Watermelon was a special treat in the summer, though I don't recall any other kind of melon. The watermelon rinds were saved and pickled (with vinegar, sugar, and a few spices, I think); this is still my favorite kind of pickle. We always had it for Thanksgiving and Christmas, and usually when there was company.

In cooking, the main condiment was of course salt; pepper was occasionally used, never paprika. For desserts, ginger and cinnamon and nutmeg were common, but for meat and vegetable cookery no herbs either fresh or dry were used, not even parsley. At the table, horseradish and mustard were the only additives. This was plain cooking with a vengeance, and extraordinarily tiresome on an everyday basis.

Most meals included some fairly rich dessert, and very good many of them were. My mother's pies were justly famous; the crusts, made with lard, were thin and pale but extremely tasty. We had pie several times every week, apple and mince and pumpkin and blueberry and cherry and rhubarb (none of these came out of cans). She was cursed however by "being no hand at a cake," which I think bothered her a lot. It bothered me too, as I had quite a sweet tooth and could be put into a state of ecstasy by the cakes some of my friends' mothers made: beaten for incredibly long periods and with incredible vigor, made in multiple layers with rich and varied frostings between, both cake and frosting feather-light in texture but heart-warmingly substantial in their essential nature, tasting of honest milk, sugar, eggs, and butter with no glutinous or antibacterial additives (preservatives were never needed with those cakes, which lasted three hours at the very most, however large)—where was I? Oh yes, saying that my mother couldn't make them. Alas....

She did make a simple one-egg, one-layer cake that was served with a thin cornstarch sauce tasting of vinegar and nutmeg, and called "cottage pudding," which I dearly loved and still do. I have recently seen this dish put down most scornfully in a book describing meals in an early-twentieth-century boarding house; well, tastes differ and my mother's tasted delicious to me, a real comfort food. She also made wonderful cookies, especially thick solid ginger cookies (eaten usually with a good slab of butter on top) and something called "fill cookies" which were large and soft, two layers of a plain sweet dough with a thick sweet raisin-and-vinegar mixture between. Two or three fill cookies and a glass of milk would hold even an adolescent boy for an hour or so, and it was noticeable as we got older that boys did tend to hang around our house in the late afternoons and after supper; I don't think it was *all* due to my sister's charms, though she was pretty cute.

The real stars of my mother's culinary repertoire were her doughnuts, for which grown men as well as boys would come sniffing around. I remember one particular Fuller Brush salesman, a tall lanky young fellow, who managed (after his first taste) to find out her doughnut-making schedule and would appear on the dot that Saturday morning. Parking his bulging suitcase on the porch, well aware that he would never make a sale in this house, he would sit in the kitchen blissfully washing doughnuts down with cold milk while she went on frying more, and on leaving would present her—to her great gratification—with a sample vegetable brush or a little whisk broom. I think these episodes were about as near as my mother ever got to flirting, and they weren't exactly that because I was right there watching and there wasn't so much as a smile exchanged. But he liked her doughnuts and she liked having her doughnuts appreciated, so there was value received on both sides. (My father liked her doughnuts too, enormously and volubly, but he was not a tall stranger; it's a little different.)

We had jelly rolls ("roll jell cake," my mother's recipe card says) and baked custards, wonderful long-baked rice puddings with raisins, gingerbread with whipped cream (you could whip the cream that came on the top of the milk, then) and my all-time favorite dessert, snow pudding (a lemon-flavored soft meringue served with a boiled custard sauce). Dessert was really worth coming to the table for, in the days before cholesterol was discovered.

And I haven't even mentioned the glory of Vermont eating, the essence of the flavor of childhood to me, maple syrup and maple sugar. We had this all the time; it was a staple. Ours came, for the most part, from my parents' old homes; we would bring back pails and cans full when we visited them and my grandparents would bring it when they visited us; but for that matter it was not very expensive in the Bennington stores either. We ate the syrup straight, with a tablespoon, out of cereal bowls, half a cup or more at a time; we boiled it until it "threaded" and then stirred it in our individual dishes until it granulated and hardened and ate that; we dribbled it on baking-powder biscuits, over the butter. We dug out the hard premade sugar from its big tin cans and spread it thickly on buttered bread for a sandwich between meals; we crumbled it onto our breakfast oatmeal and into our applesauce. We poured the syrup on pancakes of course (this was 100 percent maple syrup, sweet as sin, not the heavily diluted modern make-believes that say in very large letters PURE VERMONT MAPLE and, just beneath that in very small letters, "10 percent"). We made frostings and fudges, usually in combination with butternuts (pronounced but-nuts by the old-timers). On winter evenings with nothing special to do we set syrup to boil and packed a big dishpan with snow; when the syrup reached a stage just before true threading, we trickled it over the snow in lacy patterns, where it hardened almost to the consistency of taffy; we then used forks to twirl up great gobbets like suckers, which would take an hour or so to consume. (This confection is called "sugar on snow.")

We did have bad teeth, all of us. Most of our parents and grandparents had dentures as a matter of course; the notion that one's teeth might, with care, last a whole New England lifetime—and what proper care might consist of—would have astonished us.

I see that, by the description I have given, what my mother gave us to eat was really a fairly well-rounded and satisfactory diet; I certainly could not put meals of the same quality on the table from the same resources. And I can't deny that a great deal of it was extremely good by any standard, even reaching to gourmet heights. Yet my inner picture of that dietary, overall, is still one of monotonous, gray, heavy but unsatisfying food and just too many potatoes; and we *were* skinny kids. I think the meals of honeydew were rather few and far between; probably that is why they stand out so radiantly in my memory.

Health and Sickness

IN THAT DAY AND AGE, your health was a thing that happened to you; the idea that you had any control over it was unheard of as yet. The Lord giveth and the Lord taketh away, was the general idea—although in my own circles this would never be *said*, just as we never said "God willing" or "There, but for the grace of God" or even "Thank God"; all these were forms of taking His name in vain, we just didn't use such expressions in the secular world. The divine attributes of "Mercy" and "Goodness"—or, in the case of someone as old-fashioned as my grandmother Hulett, "My land o' Goshen"—stood in for the Divine Name among the women; most adult men kept their tongues under complete control. Country men or adolescent boys who could not control themselves used the transparent euphemisms of Darn and Dang and Ding for Damn; Gol (or Golly) for God; and Geezum (or Geeze) for Jesus; in my high school days there was a vogue one year for "Geedum crimminy." Even these were shushed by the women if they were within hearing. "Tarnation" and "Sam Hill" both meant hell, as in "what in tarnation (or what in Sam Hill) does he think he's up to now?" My father used none of the above; his closest approach to profanity was "By the great Lord Harry," of whose derivation I have no idea (but I *think* it referred to the Devil); for him, this was an expression of very strong feeling indeed, brought out when speaking of Hitler and people who got into debt or dodged their taxes (we were poor enough but what we couldn't pay for we did without; debt was a disgrace). Any expressions worse than these I never heard in my life—let alone any anatomical or sexual terminology by way of casual obscenity—*any*—until I had finished graduate school and came to live in New York

City in the 1950s. (How times have changed!)

That was a digression. I was saying that people took their health passively when I was a child. The great public-health movement of the early part of the century was just beginning to penetrate into towns like Bennington, in the form of periodic physical examinations in school and close attention to the growth of school children, chiefly aimed at ensuring that they got enough to eat. Books were starting to be written: among my parents' old schoolbooks (which constituted my well-studied home library) was one called "The Boys and Girls of Wake-up Town," circa 1912 I would say. This was all about a feeble bunch of slouching good-for-nothing eighth-graders who are transformed, I forget by what revelation, into brisk calisthenics-and-fresh-air freaks who rake their lawns and clean out their garages and, if I recall, reform the entire government of their small American town before they are through. That was where I learned about brushing your teeth for five minutes three times a day and sleeping (in a certain "hygienic" position that did not crowd your heart) a certain number of hours every night and eating perfectly inordinate (it seemed to me) amounts of fruits and vegetables. The whole regime struck me as extravagant and unnecessary and was not reinforced from any other source so it did not affect my life much except that for some years I tried to sleep so as not to crowd my heart.

In school we were weighed every month I think, and inspected by the school nurse for skin and eye infections and for lice; the school doctor looked us over every couple of years or so, otherwise most of us would never have been seen by a doctor at all. My parents were thus repeatedly informed of my underweight status, my enormous tonsils, and my need for dental care; but as I had no complaints of my own in these areas and money was always short, these messages had no noticeable result.

One kind of message did get results, and that was when every now and then the school nurse found lice in somebody's hair and sent mimeographed notices home for the whole class. This got action from agitated mothers all over town, and the children, whether infested themselves or not, knew they were in for a bad time. The treatment (and prophylaxis), at that time, consisted of a concoction of sulfur—plain yellow sulfur—mixed into a quantity of lard—plain white lard—and applied thickly, at bedtime, over the entire body surface including the scalp. To prevent loss of this potent magic, the unfortunate child had to wear a little cloth cap and a suit of long underwear. We were used to this underwear, we wore it all winter under our brown stockings, but at night we were accustomed to being free. Lard is about the greasiest substance I know of, and smelled of animal grossness; the sulfur added a sandy texture and a hellish stench of its own; and our own mothers rubbed this stuff all over us and sealed us into little isolation packages with it and said goodnight as cheerful and matter-of-fact as if they thought we were going to sleep. (We went to sleep perfectly well, I'm sure, but the minutes *before* falling asleep were consumed in a sense of helpless outrage that was not matched in my experience until, years later, I underwent my first colonoscopy.) This procedure was repeated nightly until the school authorities sounded the all-clear, usually a week or so. And if you think we got a bath every morning to wash off this horror, you are wrong. We were not bathed for any such minor reason, especially when more was to be applied the next night anyway. The only special thing that happened in the morning was that our hair was combed with a fine-tooth comb to remove any nits; having your hair fine-combed when it is full of slept-on sulfur and lard is not pleasant either. So we itched and stunk through the brilliant spring days (this seemed to happen toward the end of March, most years) and were most miserable, our only comfort being that all our friends were going through the same hideous suffering.

Another good old-fashioned remedy that was still in vogue in my day was castor oil. It is the foulest-tasting stuff I have ever put in my mouth; the gorge rises at its approach, the whole body shrinks in denial; it is *disgusting*. Two tablespoons was the usual dose—you had to do this dreadful thing twice. Now my mother read somewhere that if you mixed castor oil into a cup of warm milk and beat it with an eggbeater, it would not taste so bad. I don't know what unnatural child or wishfully-thinking adult ever attested to this proposition; for me it was quite the contrary, I felt I was drinking a whole cup full of warm and foaming castor oil. But such is the power of the printed word that my mother, in all good faith, afflicted me with several of these doses before I was able to convince her that I would *really* rather take the medicine straight.

Well, they have stopped giving castor oil to innocent children. Who says humanity does not progress?

We have progressed in other ways too. It is hard even for me to believe my own recollections of how, so short a time ago, we took for granted and simply put up with deformities, ailments, and malfunctions that would appal the modern educator. To speak only of the conditions in my own class and neighborhood, maybe forty children altogether: there was severe eczema (and when it came to adolescence, most of us had acne to a disfiguring degree), asthma (with attacks in the classroom), epilepsy (with fits in the classroom), limping due to polio, limping due to congenital dislocation of the hip, a club foot, several crossed eyes (unoperated) and broken noses (unset), mental retardation of varying but noticeable degrees, one severe and one mild cerebral palsy, two moderate cases of stuttering, and one nearly incomprehensible lisp.

We all had pretty bad dental caries, and if your teeth came in crooked or crowded that's the way they stayed. In addition to terrible colds and earaches in the winter, and ringworm, and fairly frequent styes and pinkeye, we had scarlet fever and rheumatic fever (with subsequent disabling heart disease), mastoid infections, and warts— all untreated, or at least ineffectively treated because medicine simply hadn't gotten that far. Of course we all had what were still called "the usual childhood diseases," measles, German measles (rubella), chickenpox, mumps, and often whooping cough. Two boys in our class were slightly overweight; they were called "Fatty" as a matter of course—I mean that was the name they were regularly and affectionately known by (just as the one boy in our class with decent personal hygiene and basic good manners was called "Sissy")—but no other notice, and certainly no action, was taken.

There were no social workers attached to our schools, or anywhere else in town that I know of. Nobody, child or adult, went to counsellors or therapists; psychiatrists were just beginning to be heard of, chiefly as a newfangled city phenomenon that it was smart to joke about (the point of the joke usually being the humor in the idea of looking for human help if you were "crazy"). Behind the humor lay the profound Vermont antipathy to asking anybody for help at all; you stood on your own feet, you took care of yourself, you minded your own business and kept your troubles to yourself like everybody else.

There *were* a few "crazy" people around, two of them on Silver Street itself; from my present standpoint, it seems likely that they were schizophrenic. They gave nobody any trouble, at least outside their own family, and it would not have occurred to anyone to look for treatment, or that their disorder even had a cause. Some people were crazy or "went crazy," or "queer," and that was that. They were still family members, and considerately ignored by the rest of the community, or treated with embarrassed and exaggerated politeness when it couldn't be avoided.

Nobody fussed about what we ate on the basis of our health; some mothers objected to food being left on the plate on the grounds of waste. The main concern of most housewives was putting *enough* food on the table to keep their children growing and their husbands working and themselves up to the demands of their strenuous lives; the idea of "balancing" the diet, in fact the whole concept of food groups that required balancing, had not yet arrived in Bennington. Vitamins were coming in, though: quite a few of us children were afflicted every winter by having to swallow large amounts of a thick odorous potion known as ABD Malt, on the grounds that it would prevent colds (it didn't). Sporadically, also, my mother (who read magazines from the library and I think prided herself on being up-to-date) dosed me with cod-liver oil; it was pretty bad, but not to be compared with castor oil, so I swallowed it fairly quietly.

The adults in our lives were a various lot both physically and mentally; mass culture had not yet crept in, that culture which now tells us all to Be Ourselves, and exactly what kind of Self it is good to Be, and where we can go to be whittled and pressed into the fashionable mold. In the old days, real individual differences and idiosyncrasies, untouched by medicine, therapy, exercise (or relaxation), "talking it out," or even I suspect prayer, held their serene sway inside each person and intensified with the years so that people became ever more like themselves, in fact took a certain ornery pride in their own peculiarities, which in general were accepted by their families and neighbors as simply the inherent flavor of the person and nothing to be tampered with. People were given labels early in life and tended to live up to them, as if carving themselves out of marble, progressively trimming away everything that didn't match the socially perceived persona.

I remember a couple of cases, though, where the developing person threw off the label and emerged as quite a different character; the change was received with disapproval and indignation: "I never would have known her," "He's *changed*" (spoken in a horrified sepulchral tone)—even though, to my own perception, the change was in both cases distinctly for the better.

The stubborn individuality of the "normal" Vermonter necessitated certain social adaptations which on the whole were resignedly and tolerantly applied; it made for variety of social interchange and for excellent opportunities to laugh at your neighbors. In marriage of course it presented some problems; during my childhood no divorces ever came to my personal attention, but I knew several middle-aged couples who did not speak to each other.

It was the same with physical characteristics. People were the way they were; there was none of this modern implication that there is something wrong with the way about three-quarters of us are and that it is our right, even our deepest obligation, to conform to the norm. In my day you were, and generally remained, tall or short, thin or "fleshy," weak or strong, well-formed or deformed, good-looking or not (on the whole it was more respectable to be *not*). If you were scarred, the scar stayed; if you lost a tooth, the gap remained; if you were fifty pounds overweight or "nervous," that was the cross you had to bear. You showed your character, what you were made of, by how composedly you accepted these givens, not by the strenuousness of your efforts to change them—that would have been considered entirely frivolous. And indeed, in the majority of cases there was nothing to be done. To brood about how things were, or nurse any sense of injustice or tragedy, was not socially sanctioned; you were expected to make the best of it and to exert yourself courageously as a responsible adult in spite of it. People who did this successfully were in fact highly respected; strength (of character) was universally admired, and not to be a whiner was almost the primary virtue.

Working Mother

MY MOTHER GOT UP every morning girded (metaphorically speaking) for a race. As soon as breakfast was over, dishes washed, wiped, and put away, and the kitchen floor swept, she hurried back upstairs to pull up the blinds, make the beds, wipe the bathroom floor, dust the stairs on the way down, dust the living room, take all the small rugs from upstairs *and* downstairs out on the porch, shake them, sweep them, sweep the porch itself, and bring the rugs back in. Only when these little chores had been taken care of had she achieved, in her own mind, domestic decency and the ability to look her neighbors in the face.

She was not alone in maintaining these standards. If her upstairs blinds had been seen still pulled down after nine o'clock in the morning and she herself had not been seen on the porch, illness or calamity would have been assumed by the entire neighborhood; the only alternative was moral depravity—which was unthinkable. The idea that a woman responsible for a house might just sleep late some morning for no special reason, or might just be tired after a terrific bout of canning tomatoes, would not have entered one of these ladies' minds. They wouldn't do such a thing, and they wouldn't expect anyone else to do it.

After making the place shipshape, if it was Monday the washing was the business of the day. On Silver Street the washing was done entirely by hand, in a galvanized-tin washtub supported on the seats of two kitchen chairs and filled (by means of a siphon rigged up by my father) with the hottest possible water from the sink. Strong yellow soap (Fels-Naphtha, I recall; my mother did make some soap herself on one occasion, but it was too dreadful a job even for her) was shaved with a paring knife into the hot water and the clothes were soaked for half an hour and then scrubbed by hand on a large scrub board, with repeated direct applications of soap as necessary, until they were clean. As all clothes, underwear as well as outerwear, were normally worn for a whole week between washings, they were thoroughly, deeply dirty and took a lot of scrubbing; how my mother's hands survived this weekly punishment I don't know. One of her few concessions to "beauty care" was a small bottle of Hinds' Honey and Almond Cream kept in the bathroom cabinet; but each little bottle lasted so long I can't believe she used it routinely after washing the clothes.

Periodically, once a month or so, the white clothes (this included all sheets, towels, dishtowels, and most underwear, as well as my father's shirts) received additional treatment: they were piled into a big copper boiler that sat precariously on top of a two-burner kerosene stove in the shed; the boiler was then filled with water, soap was added, and the whole thing was allowed to boil for a good half hour, during which time it was periodically stirred around with a heavy stick (I believe some women had specially shaped paddles for this purpose, but my mother used a forked stick that my father had cut and peeled for her in the woods in back of the house). No bleach was ever used, boiling water followed by hours of direct sunlight sufficing to keep most things whiter-than-white.

Stirring a three-foot-long cauldron of heavy clothes in boiling water, at shoulder level, over an open flame—especially in August—is no work for a weak woman or one of less than iron determination. Yet some women are, literally, weak; some are not endowed with either mental or physical energy to rise to this kind of challenge; how did they all get through those gruelling washdays? I think of a number of small, mild women I knew, with no more stamina than chipmunks, one would think; they managed, somehow. My own mother, though reasonably robust, often seemed tired, but she never shirked the work. ("Shirking" and "whining" were two kindred sins that you simply did not commit, in that society, as long as you were conscious; they were not excused.)

When the washing was done (each load of course had to be

rinsed with the same laborious siphon procedure for emptying and filling the washtub), it was put item by item through a hand-operated wringer to get out at least some of the water. A majority of the cotton clothes were then carried over to the stove to be dipped in a starch solution; there were several pots with different concentrations depending on whether you wanted a really board-like finish as in a man's shirt collar, or just enough crispness to prevent a little girl's skirt from wilting the minute she put it on. And some dressy items such as lace collars would be dipped in "bluing," whatever that may have been; it looked like diluted ink, and served the same purpose as a blue rinse on silver hair.

Then it was all carried out through the shed and behind the house (is your back starting to ache yet?) to be pinned up on the clothesline, where it flew in the breeze or froze in the cold most of the day for everyone to see and draw their conclusions from; after which it was all taken down again, sprinkled with water, rolled into tight cylinders and stacked in the washtub ready for Tuesday's work of ironing.

On Tuesday, after the morning chores were done, a board was arranged over the backs of the same two kitchen chairs, a good fire was built up in the stove, and two or three flatirons of cast iron were laid on its top to heat. There was one handle for all of them, a coil of wrought iron itself, that after a few minutes would get so hot it had to be wrapped in a dishtowel; it latched onto an iron or let it go by means of a tricky mechanism that I never got the hang of. My mother would test the heat of her iron by wetting her finger and touching it to the hot under-surface of the iron; she could judge accurately, by the sizzle, whether it was at the right temperature for a bit of starched lace or the sleeve of her best and only rayon blouse. The irons cooled off in use, of course, and had to be switched frequently, and the whole procedure was unspeakably cumbersome and exhausting. Nearly the whole wash had to be ironed: almost none of the clothes were of jersey-like materials, there were no synthetic fibers in any of the fabrics, and the convenient vogue for wrinkled clothing was more than half a century in the future. Sheets, underclothes, gloves, all got painstakingly pressed, and while the board was up my mother would brush off and sponge whichever of my father's two suits he was not wearing that day, and press it too. As far as I recall, nothing was ever sent to the dry cleaner's; if there was one in Bennington at all, it was certainly not patronized by my family.

After the exertions of Monday and Tuesday it occasionally happened that a woman would feel a little low, or have a bit of a headache. This was considered weakminded and unbecoming, and if she was a Vermonter, she said nothing about it, but held her mouth in an even straighter line than usual.

But how they must have looked forward to Wednesday, which was devoted to mending! Every housewife had a good-sized mending-basket and every week there would be two or three hours' work in it, after the washing was done. At least this was sit-down work, and you could invite your neighbor to come over in the afternoon bringing her own mending, and have a good talk, out on the lawn under the tree maybe, while you worked away turning collars and patching worn elbows and replacing straps and tightening buttons. Darning of stockings and socks alone took a good part of this time; most housewives of that day took the view of my grandfather Hulett, that darning of socks was well worth while up to the point where the necessary thread would cost more than a new pair of socks. (He, poor man, with a wife who was not quite up to it, darned his own socks. He could knit them, too.)

It was not uncommon, by Grandpa's rule, to see socks whose toes and heels consisted entirely of a mosaic of darns of different vintages and varying colors. I have contributed to such compositions myself, and very proud it makes you feel, to have kept a good garment going for so many useful rounds. The work was done with the help of an extremely aesthetic wooden shape called a "darning egg," over which you could drape the sock so as to steady the area of the hole, allowing a smooth reconstruction of the missing material. For this kind of mending there was a special soft thread called "darning cotton," of which every household maintained a supply in several basic colors. I tried to buy some recently, for another purpose, in a store devoted to sewing supplies, and was shocked to find it is no longer available; the middle-aged clerks had never heard of such a thing. Oh my.

It must have been on Thursdays and Fridays that my mother did her major housecleaning. For some reason that I have never understood but gladly took advantage of—maybe having to do with her own too-responsible youth—she never gave us girls any significant chores to do or initiated us into her system of domestic management. And whereas I picked up a certain amount of kitchen and laundry lore because these activities are fascinating to watch—you can see things happening, and homely materials undergoing vital transformations—I didn't give the same kind of attention at all to her cleaning activities, and came to my own domestic responsibilities years later as a complete novice, with everything to learn from scratch.

But I remember her sweeping all the floors and our one big rug in the living room several times a week; and periodically mopping floors all over the house with that same Fels-Naphtha and hot water in a pail, and a mop made of our old underclothes. Neither floors nor furniture were ever treated with any kind of polish, and naturally, over a period of time, their finish deteriorated; the general appearance of our rooms, like that of our clothing, was rather poor and bare but specklessly, relentlessly clean. (It was the same in all our neighbors' houses.) Windows were kept sparkling, and curtains, mostly of cheap lace or netting, were washed several times each season with the full copper-boiling-kettle treatment, followed by starching, drying on an unbelievable contraption called a curtain stretcher, and then mending (the cleaning and stretching procedures were hard on the delicate fabrics). Once or twice a year the big rug was, with my father's help, rolled up and lugged out to the backyard, hoisted over a couple of clotheslines, beaten furiously with the flat side of a broom, and then left to air for the whole day. The same treatment was given to the heavy blankets and patchwork woolen quilts that kept us, or tried to keep us, warm in our unheated bedrooms with the windows always open at least a crack even in zero weather.

Those icy bedrooms! The open windows were never a matter for discussion, any more than any other article of faith; you had "fresh air" to sleep by, and that was that. We slept in flannel gowns, and a little before bedtime my mother would fill a Mason jar with boiling water, wrap it in a towel, and put it down where our feet would go; it did help us to get to sleep. We had plenty of covers; they were so heavy they weighed us down and we could hardly turn over. Turning over was a bad idea anyway, since it exposed all your outlying parts to new areas of the sheet that had not been warmed as part of your cocoon. Also, unless you managed with particular care, you were apt to unbalance the whole topheavy construction of covers so that they would slide right off the bed and you would have to get out into the freezing air and rebuild them. So we held one position all night, as near as we could, and used to wake up perfectly stiff in the mornings.

The household for which my mother was responsible was hardly ever limited to the four of us. On Silver Street we had, for three or four years, teachers boarding with us; and for least two of those winters we also had Aunt Etta. She was my grandfather Hulett's sister, an elderly and emaciated widow; she lived up in Manchester, alone, in a big house with a pillared portico. When we paid her a visit she would give each of us girls a nickel, out of a pewter sugar dish she kept on a high shelf, and we thought she was as rich as Croesus. This was partly because of the nickels and partly because of the unprecedented size of her house and lawn (there was a very pretty old-fashioned flower garden right in the middle of the lawn, which was otherwise shaded by a number of old elms); and partly again because she had a certain gentle and considerate air that seemed to speak of breeding; some country people do have that natural graciousness.

It was in relation to Aunt Etta (her real name was Esther) that I learned the word "hypochondriac," because that was her occupation; or at least my mother thought so. Whatever their source, her ailments—chiefly aches and pains of the kind then lumped under the overall heading of "rheumatism"—kept her bed-bound and unable to care for herself for weeks and months at a time, and convalescent in a rocking chair for weeks and months after that; she would stay in an upstairs bedroom and my mother would bring up meals and cups of tea on trays, and wash her, and empty her chamber pot, and sit and keep her company, all that time. The same kind of episode brought her to the Warn Street house on at least three occasions, for the same wearisome sequence lasting up to half a year. I would see little of her when she was at her worst, but later I sometimes visited her room to play rummy or checkers or to have her draw me some flowers, an accomplishment she had acquired in early youth and was surprisingly skilled at.

When Aunt Etta was not with us it would be my mother's turn to have Grandma Hulett stay; and after Aunt Etta finally died, Grandma settled in permanently; she was a regular part of the Warn Street family until her death twenty years later. She could at least take care of her personal hygiene, and was also assigned the morning dusting, which took her several hours; but there was still her chamber pot to be emptied, her meals and clothing to be provided and taken care of, and her intensely aggravating company to be put up with (there was something about Grandma that put your teeth on edge; yet you had to stifle your annoyance because she was clearly not quite responsible). My mother did all this, and never failed, and never lost her temper—at least not overtly. It all came under the heading of doing your duty, and doing your duty had, at that time and place, an absolute and primary claim on your energies.

In the summer, as I have told already, regular chores were supplemented (but not displaced) by canning and jelly making on a heroic scale; these enterprises were merely sandwiched in, in the heat of August, which was especially enervating for my mother. I remember how she used to come into the relatively cool living room and lie down on the floor (there was a sofa, but the floor was cooler) in between batches of carrots or beans, for a little breathing spell.

She made all her own clothes, all her life, and my sister's and mine until we reached high school; and, though she actively disliked knitting, she knitted our caps and mittens as well (in her spare time, as it were).

Saturday was baking day, and on Sunday women were supposed to rest (except for the usual morning pickup, and preparing and cleaning up after three particularly solid meals). Sunday morning the family went to church of course, and after dinner a visit to some friend or relative was often undertaken, or just a ride in the country for several hours: south through Pownal into the Berkshires or along the Mohawk Trail; or east toward Woodford and Wilmington; or north to Wallingford or Dorset. The scenery in all directions from Bennington is extraordinarily beautiful—on a small New England scale—and my mother had a deep feeling for it; I think she derived and renewed her strength largely from these outings. Of course in October, in Vermont, a person would have to be deprived of all five senses not to feel a leaping of the spirit at the glory on the land; but for those who live there, the countryside is beautiful all the time, ever-changing and ever-constant.

I loved the country too. I loved the friendly presence of the mountains and the bumpy, meager pastures with their granite outcroppings; and I loved the sparse, dilapidated, and unpainted farm buildings inhabiting the valleys. Those old, brown, gently sagging structures held a profound romantic charm for me—they seemed to have grown organically out of the soil, or just accumulated peacefully as a natural sediment from years of quiet human occupation. When, after the Depression, people began to repair and paint their places, it struck me as a violation of the landscape; I greatly preferred the old look, homely, unaffected, and real.

Our rides often went off onto back roads, all of which my father knew from his traveling around to interview "prospects" and from his frequent hunting and fishing trips (he seemed to get his own rest and refreshment from being alone out there, away from his somewhat female-ridden home). Even with the family along, he would stop to shoot at woodchucks by the roadside whenever he saw them (his rifle always came along on any expedition in the car). A stop to fix a flat tire was also a normal event; and the condition of those dirt roads was such that we frequently went off the edges or got stuck on them, either in mud or snow. This too was taken as a matter of course; my father was all cheerful bustle and resourcefulness in getting us out, while my mother sat tranquilly in the front seat, queen for the afternoon, her mouth in a perfectly straight line, dreaming no doubt of Monday's wash to come.

I am happy to say that when we moved to Warn Street things got a little easier for her. An electric iron was acquired, and an ironing board that folded out from the wall and back into it; and an electric washing machine was installed in the cellar. This monster, a large metal cylinder on legs, filled itself from a hose connected directly to the water line, and emptied itself into a drain in the cellar floor. It had a motor-driven agitator to save all that scrubbing, and an electrically operated wringer mounted right above the tub so that dripping clothes could be fed into it. I was occasionally, in high school years, drafted for this job, and I remember how the clothes, if not manipulated with the most excruciating and foresighted skill, had a disagreeable tendency to bunch up in the middle of the wringer or get caught in the machinery on the side; but it was still a great deal better than hand wringing. This machine was my mother's pride and joy for twenty-five years, after which she acquired the by-then-standard twin white porcelain cubes in her kitchen and neither she nor my father ever had to carry tubs of wet washing up the cellar stairs again.

Eventually, also—but not until I had left home—there was a vacuum cleaner.

My mother was an intelligent, energetic, and educated woman, and in various ways led me to suspect that she might have liked a chance to prove herself in some larger arena, and against more exotic challenges, than those presented to her by circumstance. Whether for that or other reasons, there was a pervasive gloominess about her— besides the natural fatigue of her exertions—as if life had dealt her some great injury and left her no longer capable of joy, only effort. But effort she did give, in full measure; she never complained, but put everything she had of brain and muscle and imagination—not to mention courage and tolerance and plain sticktuitiveness—into the work that lay before her; and she was honored for it in her family and her community. There were many women of that mold in Bennington; and men too. It is a mold I am old-fashioned enough to find admirable still.

The Saving Grace

OUR HOUSE WAS DIFFERENT from any other house of my experience (then and since), because of my father's singing. It was not constant, of course, but the feel of it was somehow always there—like a fragrance, its memory lingered. A snatch of it would pop up from the cellar or in from the garden; when my father was shaving or wiping the dishes his music would fill the whole little house. Commonly, when he came down the stairs or around the corner or into a room and found you, he would—instead of making any conversational overture (he was not much of a talker)—strike a little comical attitude and sing you a song.

Fortunately his voice (a light, high, sweet, true tenor) and his whole personality (also sweet, gentlemanly, and retiring, yet emanating a sense of wonderful secrets to be known and bits of rare skill to be imparted, irresistible to everyone but especially to children) were such that this awareness of his presence was in no way disagreeable. On the contrary: to know that my father was in the house was to feel your spirits lift and to sense that enjoyable things would be happening. (This in strong contrast to my virtuous mother, who was working her fingers to the bone day and night in true love, but did it inside such a powerful aura of grim and anxious duty that it was sometimes quite uncomfortable to be in her presence.)

My father represented, to us children, the spirit of fun, of rare extravagance, of expressed gentleness and love. My mother was an ant to his grasshopper; recognizing this, and unable to change it, she kept to her work—without complaint, to be sure, but without apparent satisfaction either—and silently nursed the canker in her bosom. When one of us girls came home with some amazing story, my mother's response was commonly "Mirabile dictu!"—but it sounded, somehow, sarcastic and disparaging, as if our grand revelation wouldn't make any real difference to anything. But my father would listen to the same tale with raised eyebrows and open mouth, and then give a little chuckle and say "Is—that—so!" in a gratifyingly credulous tone; you felt that your point had really been taken, that you had expressed yourself unusually well, and that he was deeply impressed.

It was my father who brought home the new car (at which my mother cried because we couldn't afford it), the miraculous Victrola and later the radio, and two goldfish once (whom we named Herbert and Hoover, and who died with spots when my sister and I had the measles); he took us swimming, and to the Fish Hatchery, and made us little desks and boxes in his workshop down cellar. My mother, with endless contrivance and fatigue and worry, made ends meet and managed to feed and clothe us (in ways that we did not always appreciate because her means were so limited). She kept the family afloat. But my father—such is the terrible unfairness of life—was lovable.

He was, during our first ten years in Bennington, nominally a salesman for the Connecticut Mutual Life Insurance Company; but he didn't have the temperament for selling. In college his preferred subjects had been philosophy and poetry, and he had seriously considered being ordained. He was in no way fitted for the hustling world of business; his mind simply didn't work that way. He spent endless hours at home in scrupulous thinking about "prospects" and their needs, and working out on his old black Underwood typewriter, with painstaking care, detailed plans for their permanent security and welfare, while a brasher snappier less thoughtful rival walked off with the signature on the application.

I remember that the word "prospect," which to a salesman means only a potential buyer, meant only that to me too, all through my childhood. Mention of Prospect Mountain fifteen miles to the east of us (which later became a thriving ski resort) brought to my mind the image of a mountain rather like that surrounding the Bay of Naples, thickly built up with luxurious villas inhabited by rich people eager to buy insurance; on our occasional Sunday rides up there to enjoy the view, I would be vaguely surprised and disappointed to find it untouched by the hand of man. Prospect Street in Bennington was subject to a similar misinterpretation. And the phrase "rosy prospects"—though I think I knew by the time I came across it what it meant to the world at large—is still stored for me in the same mental compartment with "rose-breasted grosbeaks" (a common winter bird in those parts), where it forever maintains an associated image of plump, twittering, blushing creatures who can be sold to.

But I was going to tell you about my father's singing. His repertoire was distinctive. There were anthems and solos from his church work of course, which he practiced carefully and at great length at home, so that I learned a number of them by heart and came to consider them very beautiful because he sang them so beautifully. These are mostly gone and forgotten now, I imagine—although I was greatly moved, a couple of years ago, to hear in a little summer chapel in Rhode Island a lovely rendition of "The Plains of Peace," one of my father's favorite solos. I hadn't heard it in over fifty years, and recalled every word and nuance, along with vivid memories of my father at the shaving glass in our kitchen and me eating my Shredded Ralston under his elbow.

Hymns in general he would frequently sing at home, and they were a mainstay of the long car trips we made to visit one or the other set of grandparents up north. (It seems hardly reasonable, but my memory is that those trips took place most often in the dead of winter, with us two girls in the back seat wrapped up immovably in a smelly old buffalo robe lined with motheaten red plush, our feet resting solidly on two large flat pieces of soapstone that my mother had scavenged from somewhere. The night before the trip she would put these stones into the oven and keep the fire going all night; the stones would retain the heat through the whole six- to eight-hour trip.)

Also on such journeys he would bring out the popular songs of his boyhood; some, by their subject and style, would seem to have belonged to *his* father's boyhood. Many of these were the standard *Golden Book* items, "Sweet Genevieve" and "Silver Threads Among the Gold," "After the Ball," "In the Gloaming," and "Long, Long Ago." (How infinitely romantic and glamorous, and how deeply moving, I found these songs! They were the emotional literature of that period of my life, and sung by my father to penetrating effect.) A favorite of his own mother's was "Billy Boy," of which he knew all the verses. "My Darling Clementine" and of course the wartime "Hinky-Dinky Parley Voo" were ones in which we all joined. And one that I specially liked was "The Old Oaken Bucket"; the rhyming of "scenes of my childhood" with "deep tangled wildwood" still strikes me as particularly felicitous. But there were several songs that I have never heard from any other source, and in the interests of social and musical history I present them here, with unavoidable lacunae where time has worn away the words.

Two of these are specifically children's songs, which I remember from my earliest childhood, when I understood them as describing real aspects of my father's boyhood at Grandma Pitkin's. One (of which I have retained only a wisp) was about a cow in a meadow:

> Tinkle-tonkle, tinkle-tonkle,
> Hear the dum de dum de dum
> Tinkle-tonkle, tinkle-tonkle,
> Hear the cowbells chime.

(There was another verse I think, then:)

> Where the grass is short and sweet,
> There she loves the best to eat;
> Tinkle-tonkle, tinkle-tonkle,
> There she loves to eat.

It comes to me, out of the depths, that this cow was called (in the missing verse) Bessie rather than Bossy; and that my mind used to chew over the discrepancy between Bessie at her ease in a wide meadow (a Pitkin cow, obviously) and all the hardworking Bossies I knew from the Hulett farm, clambering around on rocky hillsides, their bells going not so much tinkle-tonkle as dong dong. The "friendly cow all red and white," to whom I was introduced at about the same period, was thoroughly mixed in among these pictures, though I knew very well that she was not one of *our* cows.

Another song was more didactic though equally onomatopoetic:

> Tick-tock, tick-tock, my little clock,
> He lives upon the shelf.
> He stands on three round golden legs
> And so supports himself.
> His face is always white and clean,
> His hands are always black,
> The second hand on top is seen,
> The other sits way back.
>
> "Tick-tock, tick-tock," so says my clock,
> "I'm always promptly up to time,
> Ding-dong, ding-dong, the whole day long,
> My constant warnings chime;
> Da dum de dum de *dum* de dum,
> Da-da dum de dum de dah,
> Don't loiter round the livelong day
> And (*ritardando*) waste your time away!
> (*marcato*) With steady aim your work pursue,
> Success will follow you;
> Da-da dum de dum de dah de dah
> The happy hours through.
> Tick-tock, tick-tock, I am a clock,
> You'll have to wind me up.
> For if you don't I'll have...to...stop,
> My heart...beats...cease...to...throb."

The great appeal of this little song for children of my generation (I saw it work on many besides myself) began to be lost when electrically-powered clocks got to be the norm; having to have it explained spoils half the fun.

A third song, of delightfully ambiguous meaning, was:

One little maiden with black eyes,
One little maiden with blue,
Adding the maidens together
Makes two.
One little maiden's a darling,
I'm sure that the other is too,
But whether I best love the black eyes
Or blue
Will never be known for the telling,
For even supposing I knew,
I never would whisper the secret,
Would you,
Would you?

What the ages of these "little maidens" are remains for ever un-known, like the identity of the singer: is he their father? a little boy of their own age? or are they really not little girls at all, but practi-cally grown up, and the singer some stalwart Lothario with shoulders and a mustache, bent on attaching and deceiving them both? How I loved this song, which my father sang with a killing amount of sen-timental emphasis.

I am reminded, by the theme of competitive love, that my mother too sang to us, at bedtime, in our very early days, though she had no voice and no real music in her. She sang "Sweet and Low," whose refrain "while my little one, while my pretty one, sleeps" seemed to me to refer very clearly to my sister and me, and to indi-cate just as clearly that—since I was certainly the little one—Frances must be the pretty one. This hurt me quite a lot. And she sang "Bye-low, Baby Bunting," which carried conviction since my father did go a-hunting fairly often; the song kept me in apprehension of his coming home some day and wrapping me up forcibly in a great dis-gusting rabbit skin (as big as the buffalo robe but even hairier, with long ears at one end, I thought), which did not seem to me a desir-able thing. And my mother sang "Rock-a-Bye Baby" and thus planted the seed of my oldest repetitive nightmare, that of tumbling over and over, together with her, down through the infinite leafy branches of an enormous tree. (When I read some years later about the great world-tree Yggdrasil I felt I knew all about it, from way back; the myth rang absolutely true.)

And while we are down here in the murky subconscious, what about those "little men" of my mother's, who haunted me night and day for my first six or seven years? They derived from a number of sources. "Up the airy mountain, down the rushy glen, I daren't go a-hunting for fear of little men" was one, out of her big book *Children's Literature;* it really scared me. Rumpelstiltskin of course was another; in *Children's Literature* he was not even presented as a *human* little man but as a kind of black demon called That:

"Is your name…Elbert?"
"Noop, 'tain't," said That; and That twirled That's tail.

…it still makes the prickles rise on my arm. "That" spoke with an accent unnervingly suggestive of my grandfather Hulett's.…Then there was the renegade old man in Mother Goose who "wouldn't say his prayers"; that put him beyond the pale of good society no doubt, but being thrown down the stairs *by the left leg* (a fiendish touch) was surely excessive and unusual punishment; would that be done to me, if I ever forgot to say my own prayers—as was only too likely? And finally, when I was dropping off to sleep at night I could *hear* a little man walking along an endless dusty road, as it might be the road right outside my window, dup…dup…dup. I would change positions to make him go away, but in an instant he would be coming on again, dup…dup…dup, unhurried but unstoppable, sinister, white-bearded, bent over, with his pack over his back.

Much is preached in these educated days about the importance of avoiding disturbing images with young children. But if these relatively innocent songs and stories could affect me as they did (they affected my sister not at all, I found when we compared notes a few years ago), one must conclude that some children simply have dark spaces in their minds that are actively searching for dark images to match; it would be almost impossible to present material "clean"

enough for that kind of mind. Anyway, none of my father's songs affected me that way; he sang them so lightly, so fondly and pleasantly,
that even songs of unrequited love were transmuted out of sadness
into beauty. My poor mother had, somehow, a different touch.

The songs of unrequited love, besides those I mentioned before,
included "Tessie," where the course of true love was at least a little
muddied:

> Tessie is a maiden with a sparkling eye,
> Tessie is a maiden with a laugh,
> Tessie doesn't know the meaning of a sigh,
> Tessie's lots of fun and full of chaff.
>
> But sometimes we have a little quarrel, we two,
> Tessie always turns her head away;
> Then it's up to me to do as all boys do,
> So I take her hand in mine and say:
>
> "Tessie, you know I love you dearly,
> Why don't you turn around?
> You know (da dum de dum de) nearly,
> My heart weighs about a pound,
>
> Don't blame me if I ever doubt you,
> You know I couldn't live without you,
> Tessie, you are the only only o-o-o-nly.

(This seems a rather lame ending, but that's how I remember it.)

Then there was "My Jersey Lily," which I decided many decades
later must of course have been inspired by Lily Langtry, but which at
the time I understood without any question to refer to a young lady
from *New* Jersey:

> 'Mid the Jersey hills there lives a little maiden,
> No flower is fairer, no gem is rarer,

And my heart with love for her is overladen,
And I fancy that she's rather fond of me.
But like all the girls she dearly loves to tease me,
She keeps me waiting, it's aggravating,
[Dah de dah de dah de dum de dah de] please me,
So I softly take her hand in mine and say,

"My Jersey Lily, with eyes so blue,
No other Lily can equal you!
Will you be mine, dear? Please don't decline, dear,
My Jersey Lily, say you love me true."

There was one drinking song, with a lovely liquid melody that rose and fell; I suppose he picked it up in college:

Now poets may sing of the dear Fatherland
And the soft-flowing dreamy old Rhine,
Beside the blue Danube in fancy they stand
And rave of its beauties divine.
But I know a spot where the sun never shines,
Where mirth and good fellowship reign;
For dear old Bohemia my lonely heart pines
And I long to be there once again:

Take me down, down, down where the Würzburger
    flows, flows, flows,
It will drown, drown, drown all your troubles and cares
    and woes,
Just order two seidels of lager or three,
If I don't want to drink it please force it on me,
For the Rhine may be fine, but a cold stein for mine,
Down where the Würzberger flows!

The Rhine by moonlight's a beautiful sight,
When the wind whispers low through the pines,
But give me the good old Rathskeller at night

Where the brilliant electric light shines!
Now poets may think it's delightful to hear
The nightingale piping his lay,
Give me a piano, a cold stein of beer,
And a fellow who knows how to play!

Take me down, down, down, etc.

From well before the turn of the century (and where he can have found it I have no idea), this really wonderful round:

Hark to the street cries in the noisy city,
Louder and louder they fall upon the ear.
—Right this way sir, take a carriage—
—Apples, peanuts, cakes, and pies—
—Oh here's your nice sweet oranges—
—The Adams House close by—
—Bring out your old clothes—here's your fresh fish—
—FIRE FIRE FIRE—
—Tribune, Times, Evenin' Joinal—Five o'clock an'—
—Auction, auction—milk below—
—Can you tell me sir when the ten o'clock train goes—
—Mister black your boots—oh I've lost my watch—
—Hurry up!

As I said, I never heard any of these songs except from my father, so of course I never heard this, at home, in its full cacophonous glory as a round. But I kept it in my head and taught it to my three children; by the time they were preadolescent we could put on quite a good performance. We regaled my father with it once on a visit and he was tickled, as we used to say, almost to death.

And then—this must have been a college acquisition too—there was a ragtime piece which in my mind made a pair with Mr. Cummings's "Oceana Roll" (which I did hear sung in an old movie once, some years ago). This one I've never heard:

Oh, a happy little chappy at the club one day
Had nothing at all to do
So he wrote a little ditty in a ragtime way
And sang a verse or two.
And the other little chappies when they heard that song
They said "It is gr-eat, by Gum!"
And they all joined in and sang like sin,
Ze zizzy ze zum zum zum
Zee——
Zizzy ze zum zum, zizzy ze zum
That was the rag refrain,
Zizzy ze zum zum, zizzy ze zum
It drove them all insane.
From the yappy of the chappy to the deep basso
Of the raggety-tag old bum
The whole place rang with the rattlety-bang
Of zizzy ze *zee* ze zum zum, ziz*zee* ze zum zum,
Zizzy ze zum zum zum.

My father knew no classical music at all, nothing beyond hymns, anthems, and the popular songs and war songs of his youth. Even after we got the Victrola we never had more than a very few records, mostly children's songs; the only classical ones were John McCormack singing "My Wild Irish Rose," Amelita Galli-Curci (whose name we thought was hilarious) singing something I don't remember, and a rendition of the sextet from *Lucia*. So the music I heard at home was on no very exalted artistic level. It was real music nonetheless and, projected through my father's taste, his beautiful voice, and the invincible sweetness of his nature, it blessed my growing-up. My sister and I were singularly lucky to have had, woven into the plain gray rectitude of our Protestant heritage, that silver thread of sunny lightness, a little Mozart in the midst of all that Bach. And we knew it.

My father wrote poems, too, on any and all occasions, rather long and rather formal, using old-fashioned "poetical" words and

straining the syntax fearfully to fit the meter. The flattered recipient
of such an effusion would treasure it forever; I still have the poem
my father composed for my college graduation, and one that came
with a checkerboard he had made for me in his workshop, as well as
one written to my mother when "our two rosy girls" were both tod-
dlers. These poems gave expression to a deep vein of sentimentality,
which was probably a healthy foil to our otherwise laconic interac-
tions, and which certainly had us all wiping our eyes and swallowing
self-consciously at most significant family gatherings.

I will quote only one of his productions, an atypical one at that.
He used to wake us up on school mornings by striking a pose in the
doorway of our bedroom and declaiming with fervor:

> Let us then be up and doin'
> With a heart for any fate,
> For your feet you must be shoein'
> And your food you must be chewin'
> And you know that you are due in
> School at eight.

I still think that is rather neat.

There was, finally, a little counting-rhyme he taught us; he said it
was "counting to fifty in Indian" (I of course assumed, as a child,
that he meant American Indian—I hardly knew the other kind ex-
isted), and that he got it from his older brother Fred.

> Een teen tether fether fimp,
> Latter catter doe def dick,
> Eendick, teendick, tetherdick, fetherdick, BUMP!

This was said to mean:

> One two three four five,
> Six seven eight nine ten,
> One-ten, two-tens, three-tens, four-tens, FIFTY.

•

Of course I passed this on to my children too; and many years later one of my daughters sent me from college a magazine article quoting a number of variations on this rhyme, none identical but all fully recognizable. According to the article, the rhyme is found worldwide in one form or another, among the most widely separated human communities. And what I found of hair-raising interest was the claim that there is evidence that it originated in *India*. I have never seen it written down except for that article, and never met anyone outside my own family who knew it. It came to me, as it has apparently come to a host of others, as a strictly oral tradition, complete with a correct account of its source. It would seem that my roots go, not only far back, but practically all the way back.

As of course everybody else's do too.

And on that note—farewell, cousin.